A VERY ALTERNATIVE COAST TO COAST

Written by Peter Kay
Edited by E. Rachael Hardcastle

ISBN: 978-1-7399188-2-8

Edited by E. Rachael Hardcastle
Formatted by E. Rachael Hardcastle
Written by Peter Kay

Published by Curious Cat Books, United Kingdom. For further information, contact www.curiouscatbooks.co.uk

Also available as an e-book.

First Edition

This book is dedicated to anyone who has ever set out on a journey, without being clear about its final destination.

To Sally
Enjoy their journey

OTHER TITLES BY PETER KAY

A Pennine Way Odyssey self-published in 2012

Show Me The Way To Santiago published by Curious Cat Books in 2020

ACKNOWLEDGEMENTS

First and foremost, I would like to salute John and Simon for undertaking most of the journey described in this book with me and in so doing, having the odd mishap befall them. These events became the inspiration for me writing the story. I would like to thank John for his patience in reading and re-reading early versions and for his guidance on several matters of content.

I should like to give special mention to a number of fellow writers who shared in and commented on the story as it evolved, in particular: Brian, Kate, Sally, Tom, Chris, Irene and Pam. Without your encouragement, I might not have persisted with the project.

I should also like to thank my youngest daughter, Jenny, for her help with cover design and for her (and husband Kevin's) help in resolving the IT problems I encountered along the way.

I would particularly like to thank my Editor and Publisher, E. Rachael Hardcastle of Curious Cat Books for her patience and support, but most of all for her belief in me as a writer.

Finally, no book ever gets written without the support of close family, who get ignored for long periods, whilst I am ensconced writing. I would like to thank Sandra, whose understanding and support is truly appreciated.

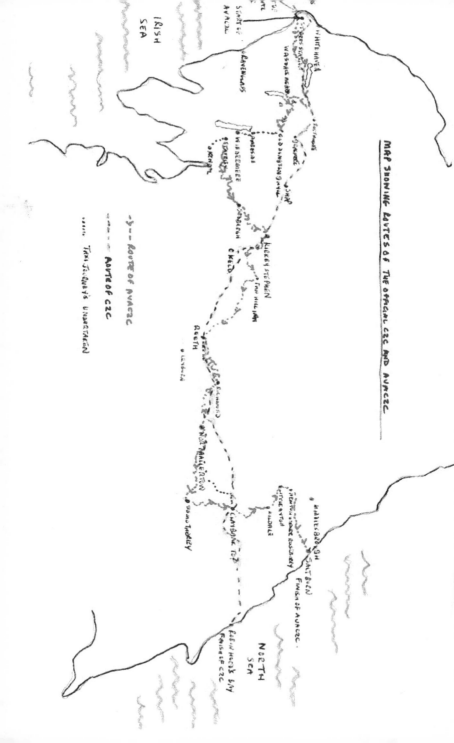

MAP SHOWING ROUTES OF THE OFFICIAL C2C AND AVAC2C

IRISH SEA

NORTH SEA

---→--- ROUTE OF AVAC2C

--•--•-- ROUTE OF C2C

·········· TRANSFER/BUS'S UNDERTAKEN

WHITEHAVEN

WORKINGTON

WASDALE HEAD

RAVENGLASS

SEASCALE

KESWICK

OLD DUNGEON GHYLL

GRASMERE

AMBLESIDE

WINDERMERE

KENDAL

KIRKBY STEPHEN

TAN HILL INN

REETH

LANGTON

RICHMOND

NORTHALLERTON

OSMOTHERLEY

CATTON ROAD

KILDALE

GREAT AYTON

GUISBOROUGH

EASTON & SHAKE BOUNDARY

WHITES BRIDGE

SALTBURN
FINISH OF AVAC2C

ROBIN HOOD'S BAY
FINISH OF C2C

PROLOGUE

The rain was lashing down, coming from the landward side, as they trod the path along the cliffs. So torrential was the barrage that many rivulets were flowing over the edge. The wind, however, was coming from the seaward side, whipping up the tumbling water droplets and hurling them back at the three bedraggled figures. It felt like walking through the jets of a car wash. They were on the last leg of the Cleveland Way, covering the ten and a half miles from Scarborough to Filey. The three had walked the rest of the route on two previous trips to the area. Today would see them finish what had been a rather splendid walk. They had a B&B booked and a meal in Filey to look forward to in the evening, but first, the three walkers had to endure the elements as they made their way along the exposed cliff top track.

Walking usually provided opportunities for them to catch up with each other's news. Two of them would walk together, deep in conversation, whilst the third forged ahead. All three occasionally walked side-by-side to play a part in their shared dialogue. Today, conversation of any kind was out of the question, as the force of the gale and the amount of water in the air left them all bowed and solely intent on maintaining both equilibrium and some forward momentum.

Each had a packed lunch stored somewhere in the bowels of their rucksacks, hidden by the colourful but sodden rain covers; blue, orange and red. Today, they would remain buried until the sanctuary of some hostelry could be reached. As at twelve and then 1pm, no-one felt the urge to suggest a cliff top lunch stop. Once, maybe twice, they formed a huddle to wrestle bottles from each other's sacks and drink water.

"Grim, isn't it?"

"Bloody awful."

"Only about another hour until Filey."

This was the longest exchange they managed during the four and a half hours they walked along the way.

They struggled on towards Filey, before dropping into the town where the outskirts gave way to terraced streets and large Victorian houses perched high above, but all looking down upon the rain lashing the promenade and seascape below. At the end of one terrace, a pub suddenly presented itself and the three stumbled over the step and ducked inside to escape from the incessant rain. Several people sat at tables eating food and drinking beer; at their feet, puddles formed. Whilst searching for the toilets, James found a row of hooks, most adorned with the outer layers of those within. A larger puddle beneath them was being fed by constant dripping from the apparel. He shared his find with the others.

The three then had to assist each other to be rid of their 'so-called' waterproof layers, which filled the remaining hooks and increased the rapidity of the dripping and the size of the pool below.

"Well, we made it," suggested Mick.

As the beers flowed and the prospect of hot showers and a change into dry clothing at the B&B was reflected upon, Andy hesitantly asked, "What's the next challenge, then?"

Andy had a young family at home and therefore full weekends were now precious; he suggested the group should limit their escapades to a maximum of two days, with an overnight sandwiched between them. They should take one of these days from the weekend. The other would be a day off from work.

"Okay," said James, "that's the first ground rule for the next challenge sorted. Let's tog up, find the B&B, and then we can all get ready to go out. We can discuss the rest of our plans over food."

Dinner was in a reasonably priced, satisfactory Italian restaurant, with a rather splendid red wine to add to the earlier beers. By the time puddings arrived, the three were in a mellow mood as the conversation turned again to 'future challenges'.

"Okay," said James, "we have one ground rule. Are there any others that need to be factored into the equation?"

"We'll need to get to the start of day one's walk by public transport," ventured Mick.

"And get back from the end of day two's walk in the same way," suggested Andy.

"Are we looking at a Friday and Saturday, then?" James asked.

Andy agreed, "That would work best for me."

"Is it a one-off challenge or a linear route we could do in stages?" asked James.

He knew it had become his role within the group to organise the itinerary, book any accommodation, resolve travel arrangements, and determine the route for any proposed walks. He was keen to be clear about what he needed to research before he presented proposals to the other two. He was also aware future 'challenge walks' would need to be discussed at a meeting of the 'committee'. Basically, this was a rouse for the three to meet up between challenges to catch up and have a few beers (as well as firming up on dates and ideas for the next challenge).

Mick said, "A walk in several stages may be best."

In response, Andy was 'easy either way'.

Conversation moved on to what was happening at work and who had left. Andy was usually the one with his finger on the pulse. Updating his work colleagues gave him centre stage within the group. Children and grandchildren were discussed before the end of the evening and it was not until they were on the train back in the morning that James reminded them to agree a date to meet up and discuss the next challenge—and to set dates for the first stage of it.

A date six weeks hence was agreed upon, and Mick and James agreed to meet Andy in Leeds, which was easier for them all at the end of a day's work.

"Great, that will give me time to follow up some ideas and work out the details," said James.

"Why, have you got an idea already?" Andy asked.

"I just wondered whether there was a way you could undertake a coast-to-coast walk using the parameters we have set?" James replied.

"Could be interesting," Mick added.

"I like that idea," said Andy.

"Well, it will give me something to work on between now and the 9th of November," said James. Already, he was questioning whether such a venture within the ground rules they had agreed to would prove workable. "It might end up being a very alternative coast to coast," he added, trying to build in some wriggle room.

CHAPTER ONE

They stand on the platform of St Bees Station at 10.15am. For James and Mick, it has been over four hours since they boarded the train at Leeds. Andy joined them at Skipton after his early morning of panic and chaos. The taxi that was supposed to come at 5.30am to take him across the hill from Otley to Leeds had not appeared. In a flap, he'd persuaded Melissa, his wife, to drive him to catch the train. However, realising that getting to Leeds in time would be extremely challenging, they drove at speed to Skipton instead, arriving two minutes before the Carlisle train was due to depart.

Mick hopes to persuade Andy to stop for a take-out coffee on the way, but the change in circumstances— texted whilst he and James were on the train— dissuades him. Mick is therefore not in the best of moods on the journey up to Carlisle, having missed his early morning fix.

Andy is fearful Melissa will wreak some terrible revenge for being dragged out of bed (literally, if he is to be believed) in order to get him to link up with his two walking buddies. Her presence always seems to dog Andy on their walks, much as it relieves him to join up with his two companions.

At least they have time at Carlisle Station to grab a coffee and a slab of cake before boarding the Barrow train, now pulling slowly away. By the time they reach

Carlisle, Andy says he is feeling less concerned about home. He has received a text from Melissa, hoping he has a good two days. The coffee and cake improve Mick's mood, too.

***

"Which way then?" asks Mick, directing the question at James, who has been responsible for planning the excursion and the route they'll follow over the next two days.

"Well," says James, "it will be a long day's walk from here to Wasdale Head, so we could forget going down the path to the sea and just head inland. After a couple of miles, we will follow the official Coast to Coast route until we get to the Black Sail Hut and then leave the route by going over the pass into Wasdale."

"What, start a Coast-to-Coast walk without visiting the actual coast?" says Andy, clearly unimpressed.

"I only said we could. If you want to, we can walk to St Bees Head and then retrace our steps or even follow the official route from there, although that would add a couple of miles more."

"Hang on a minute," says Mick, "how far is it from here to Wasdale Head?"

"About twenty-four or twenty-five miles," says James, quickly, as if doing it that way might make it seem less.

"Bloody hell!" says Mick. "What time are we going to get to the Wasdale Head Inn?"

"Between seven and eight o'clock in the evening,"

says James, secretly hoping his calculations are accurate.

"How far would it be if we went down to the sea?" asks Andy, already resigning himself to an answer that will almost certainly rule out such an essential 'deviation'.

"About a mile, so a couple of miles there and back," says James. "If you follow the official route from St Bees Head, you're adding a further four miles to our day's walk."

"Well, I vote we head east from here," says Mick.

James looks at both Andy and Mick and knows they are disappointed, but that they will agree. Mick always plays the peacemaker, once he's had his coffee fix, anyway.

"From here it is," says Mick.

"What about you, Andy?" James asks.

"Seems that heading east is the only sensible way forward. Lead on."

***

The three head off, with James scrutinising the map closely to work out how they will negotiate the next half an hour until they cross the A595 and pick up the road to Cleator, when his navigating skills will be less required (assuming the official route is well marked). He also knows the sea is only half a mile away from the station, but that had he been completely honest on that point, the likelihood is they would have headed there and probably added another 40 minutes to the day's walk.

15

Whilst they have walked similar distances to today's in a day before, they usually set off walking much earlier. As it is, the discussion on the platform adds a further five minutes, and he is angry with himself for not resolving the matter on the train. He had suggested it would be around twenty miles when they met to plan the walk, and it was only after carefully researching the route he realised it was nearer twenty-five miles. This was more like one of their earlier challenge walk days, ones they previously agreed should be consigned to history in favour of shorter distances, and more time spent in the pub catching up and reminiscing.

Mick is inwardly fuming, albeit no-one will know. Even without the additional visit to the coast, twenty-five miles is much further than he wants to be walking. He knows James well enough to know if he says twenty four to twenty five miles, it will be twenty-five, and seven to eight o'clock means James believes it will be nearer eight when they get to the Wasdale Head Inn. Given they will all need a shower and change, they will do well to be dining by nine. He'll need at least a couple of hours after eating before trying to get to sleep. It is as if the day has already become a route-march like some of their earlier challenge walks. He shrugs his shoulders, and this reminds him of the weight of the rucksack on his back and that he usually asks James to adjust the straps for him before setting off, then again after each rest stop. He wonders how many of those they will manage today.

"James, would you mind just adjusting my straps?"

"Of course, I'd forgotten to." He smiles up at Mick,

hoping he'll be forgiven for the length of the day's walk and his dishonesty at the station.

***

"Do we turn left or right?" asks Andy, for they have arrived at a crossroads of small lanes, but the junction is minus any signposts to guide them.

"Right," James says with a cursory glance at the map, which is enclosed in a waterproof carrier. He hasn't a clue, but at this early stage of the walk, he needs his companions to have full trust in his navigational skills. He believes either way will eventually deliver them to the A595.

Andy is inwardly focussed on life at home. Will Melissa remember Millie needs to be at swimming at 11.00am? He debates texting a reminder, but knows she'll take it the wrong way. He mentioned it yesterday, and on the morning dash to Skipton, so it is not as if he hasn't done his bit. He also got Millie's swimming bag ready and put it on the kitchen table where it will be visible to all. Even though Millie loves the water, her lesson will probably not be the focus if she picks up her latest Harry Potter book and starts reading. If he was there, he would both limit such activities and take her to the baths himself. If Melissa gets involved in something else at home, she'll forget.

"So, what highlights should we look out for today, James?" he asks, as much to take his mind off home as to discern what may lie ahead. James has taken time to study the route and any specific features that may interest them.

"Well, Cleator's the first proper village we will come to, so there may be a tea shop there, if we've time. Once there, we will be on the official route and have a climb up over Dent Hill before we drop to Nannycatch Beck, which is supposed to be quite a picturesque valley. We carry on to Ennerdale Bridge, which should be our lunch stop. After there, we walk along the right-hand side of Ennerdale Water and then up to Black Sail Hut, the remotest youth hostel in the Lakes, before we go up and over Black Sail Pass before dropping to Wasdale Head."

"Sounds easy when you describe it in a couple of sentences," says Mick dryly, quickly adding in a more even tone. "A tea shop in Cleator sounds most appealing."

***

It is 11.30am when the A595 is crossed, and they are following a sign that proclaims, 'Cleator: two and a half miles.'

If there is a tea shop, it does not reveal itself, although the village has some redeeming features, the parish church of St Leonard's being one. Of more interest to all three, though, is the clear Coast to Coast sign directing them between two houses and across the river Ehen, towards Blackhow Farm and beyond that, Blackhow Wood. They can see Dent Hill rising in the distance beyond.

It secretly relieves James there is an absence of a tea shop; at this stage of the walk, they don't need any undue time delays. Mick is resigned to drinking coffee from his flask, whilst hoping at the very least Ennerdale Bridge should provide somewhere to get a proper coffee.

On the ascent of Dent Hill, the three encounter a group of four fell walkers, all adorned in an assortment of brightly coloured outdoor wear. They are a motley crew, though, with their 'leader'—a slender woman, who is well ahead of her entourage, sporting a floral headband, expensive-looking walking breeches and a red jacket. She is clearly comfortable on the fells and stops to exchange greetings and query whether they are walking the coast-to-coast, and whether Ennerdale Bridge or Black Sail Hut will be the overnight stopping place.

It amazes her when she's informed by James, "We are staying at the Wasdale Head Inn tonight. Our coast-to-coast walk will follow a different route from Wainwright's."

Looking beyond James to Andy, who is bringing up the rear and not enjoying the pull up Dent, she casts a doubtful eye first to James, and then to Mick.

"Good luck," she says, smiling at Mick in a way that means, 'you'll need it'.

The second member of the group is a man of a similar age to 'floral headband'. He is a little overweight and clearly struggling to keep pace with her. He has discarded his walking jacket, which is tucked across the back of his rucksack, and is wearing a Genesis t-shirt over a pair of green walking shorts. His stout walking boots have one yellow and one red lace threaded through. He has a walking pole in each hand and grunts, 'good morning, see you've met the wife' as they pass. He has no time or energy to get involved in further conversation as he strives to keep up with his partner.

The third and fourth members of the group, a man and a woman, are both older by about fifteen to twenty years. He wears a bright green jacket, a beret and navy-blue jeans; his companion a turquoise walking jacket, yellow bandana and sandals. If they didn't stop to confirm they were with the other two, they might have been taken for a separate couple.

It impresses Mick that the older man, of similar age to himself, is wearing walking shorts and that his companion is in sandals. It vindicates his own attire. Mick's go-to apparel for his various trips with Andy and James were walking shorts, sandals and heavily tinted sunglasses to complete the 'Mister Cool' look. He is wearing the usual items today, with his heavier walking boots tied to his rucksack, along with a designer waterproof jacket.

***

The conversation of the three turns to walking attire as they continue up the hill to the large summit cairn, which affords not only good views, but an opportunity for a short stop for each to grab a drink of water and for James to consult the map. Both the rucksack and the designer waterproof Mick has with him belong to his wife, Louise.

"She buys such expensive items, whilst I make the most use of them to justify their being purchased."

Given the time of year, June, both James and Andy

are also wearing shorts, albeit they are both in boots rather than sandals. James is the only one using a walking pole—a present from his nephew—after they climbed Haystacks together some seven years ago.

Andy, Mick and James have undertaken several challenge walks together and some days, particularly in the earlier times, walking was both physically and mentally challenging. Approaches to challenges have mellowed over the years, and now they build in evenings and overnights to chill, unwind, dine well, and have a beer or two. The three have worked together for a good number of years and the challenges started about fifteen years ago. James plans to retire in four years and Mick has around six years to go. Andy is the oldest by two years, but Melissa is ten years his junior and with a younger family as well, he may need to work for some time yet. As well as nine-year-old Millie, he also has another daughter, fourteen-year-old Claire.

Setting off again, the three head down the deep declivity of the grassy path, depositing them at Nannnycatch Gate. This marks the way into the valley which meanders along the course of the beck, between the rocky screes of Flatfell to the left and wooded ground to the right. Once or twice, they must ford the beck as their path twists north-eastwards, trying to find the most level way forward, before they emerge on to a metalled road near to Kinniside Stone Circle.

On another day, James would herald the location of the Stone Circle, particularly as Mick is keen on such ancient monuments. He knows full well, if he did, they would deviate there to explore the area for a little while before continuing their walk. James hurriedly hastens them forward along the road before Andy or Mick have time to spot the sign to the Stone Circle. Not for the first time, he feels pangs of guilt at his behaviour. He rationalises both Mick and Andy accepted the challenge when he described it to them. They both knew today would be a long walk and have entrusted him with delivering them to their resting place in time to enjoy the rest of the evening (and a beer or two).

The sun has been playing hide and seek with them for most of the morning, and apart from a brief stop in Cleator and the stop at the Cairn on Dent Hill, they've made good progress.

"About half an hour to Ennerdale Bridge," volunteers James, just as all are feeling the hunger pangs a lunch stop might assuage.

Andy and Mick are deep in conversation. Mick is playing devil's advocate as Andy offloads his anxieties about whether to agree with Melissa's suggestion for a fortnight's holiday to the Algarve. He isn't sure they can afford the trip, but he hates having to play the bad guy all the time.

"We've had two holidays this year," says Andy, "and whilst I enjoy them too, as do our kids, we simply can't afford another one. Melissa had a part-time job in a shop in Otley once Millie started nursery, but that's now finished."

"It can be hard. I know Louise and I used to row about money, but now we seem to sit down and have a calm discussion. Have you tried talking to Melissa about money?"

"She just flies into a rage. Such a conversation just

doesn't go anywhere. I know she isn't happy, and I try to help all I can. She wants to be fulfilled as a person with a career role, but isn't sure what she wants to do and how to go about this. She can't talk to her parents, and she doesn't have any close friends to confide in. Anything I say is wrong."

Mick is quiet for a while before he says, "Well, I know you are very fond of Melissa and from what I have seen of the two of you together, she is equally fond of you."

This last sentence brings a smile to Andy's face. "Ah, it's just me worrying about something and nothing as usual." He sighs and shrugs. "I'm sorry, Mick, I shouldn't offload."

"The three of us don't get together very often and you know you can always use the opportunity to chew the cud on anything that's bothering you. Don't forget, we both knew you before you and Melissa got together, and no relationship ever runs perfectly all the time."

***

As the road reveals the outskirts of Ennerdale Bridge ahead, James looks at his watch: 1.30pm. Half an hour lunch-stop here, and they might get to Wasdale Head by 7pm, he thinks. A thought he decides not to share with the others. Their route through the village doesn't take them past any tea shops or indeed any pubs, although they pass a sign to the Fox and Hounds. A little park with a rounded boundary wall at a corner of which sits a bench just big enough for three provides the luxury of a sit down for a whole half hour.

Sandwiches, savouries, fruit and energy bars, supplemented with water and hot coffee from flasks, finally sate appetites sharpened by the morning's endeavours. The sun shines, though the temperature is more like April than June.

"By my calculations, we've covered nine and three-quarter miles," says James.

Another fifteen to go then, thinks Mick.

Even if they keep up the pace, it still means it will be 7pm at the earliest before they get there. He is weary at the prospect.

"Well, we better get going again," says Andy, not wanting them to lose the opportunity to arrive closer to 7pm than 8pm.

Mick feels much better for the rest, food, and the coffee, even though it is from his thermos.

CHAPTER TWO

The three tog-up again as the sun disappears behind gathering clouds and set off out of the village following the sign to Ennerdale Water. They traverse the perimeter of a large car park at the end of the lake and follow the rocky path that clings mostly to the water's edge.

"There are options on a clearer day to either climb Haycock and then follow a ridge walk over Great Scoat Fell to Wind Gap before descending to Wasdale Head. Or," he pauses, "take a route that climbs to our right at the other end of the lake to ascend Steeple. You can then go over Great Scoat Fell or go over Pillar and drop to the high point of Black Sail Pass," says James.

"Are any of those options any quicker?" asks Mick.

"They're shorter," says James, "but involve more climbing and possibly some scrambling. They also present more navigational challenges, as paths are less well trodden. Looking at the gathering cloud, even though it hasn't forecast rain, the higher summits look to be shrouded in mist, so I would prefer we stick to the clearer route. What do you two reckon?"

"I'd rather get to Wasdale Head in one piece," Mick says.

"Let's just keep going," adds Andy, feeling better for having shared his worries with Mick and to be now enjoying the walk.

It amazes him how on every one of their walks

together, he simply gets informed by text where to link up and at what time by James. He doesn't need to think too much about the route, either. James usually has that covered and will have sorted their overnight accommodation.

The underfoot conditions by the lake are tricky as the path winds its way through rock strewn terrain, with larger boulders to find a way round too. The path climbs upwards and away from the water on a couple of occasions, as continuing straight ahead would involve scrambling over small areas of scree. At the second of these climbs, Mick decides that, to save time, he will carry straight on by the water's edge and indulge in a little boulder hopping.

"On your head, be it," shouts Andy, which within thirty seconds he is regretting.

Mick half slides and half tumbles from a rock and ends up face forwards in the lake.

"Shit!" He cries out, just before he hits the water. He picks himself up, looking shaken and wet, as both James and Andy move as quickly as they can.

"My sunglasses! I can't find my sunglasses; they must have pinged off my head when I fell."

He was wearing them perched on top of his head rather than on his face, and had been since they stopped for lunch. It was a Mick thing, and both James and Andy were used to it.

"Are you alright though? That's the main thing!" James asked.

"My favourite pair and a bloody expensive pair, too. No, I'm not bloody alright," responds Mick, who is now bent double, combing the bed of the lake with his hands near the scene.

As Andy joins him at the water's edge, he can see Mick's shorts are soaked, his legs are both muddy, and there is some blood oozing from his right knee. His sandals are sodden, too. Mick seems oblivious to this as he continues in vain to locate his sunglasses. As James had been further up the path that bypasses the scree area, he is the last to arrive on the scene.

"Bloody hell, Mick. We need to get you to safer ground, and you need to change into some dry gear. It might be June but it's not that warm today."

"We need to clean up that knee, too," adds Andy, knowing somewhere in the bowels of James's rucksack will be a first aid kit.

Mick protests and wants to keep on searching for his sunglasses but recognises his friends are both right.

"Fuck, fuck, fuck," he explodes.

"Feel better? Now, let's get further up and away from here to some firmer ground where we can sort you out."

Mick takes James's advice and the three of them gingerly negotiate their way across the rest of the scree until they regain the footpath and can take stock.

"Well, at least your backpack didn't get wet, so any change of clothes will be dry," says Andy.

An antiseptic wipe cleans up the wound, which seems to have stopped bleeding, and James puts a plaster in place. Mick reluctantly changes out of both shorts and sandals and after about ten minutes, they are finally on the move again, with Mick now in long walking trousers and boots. His rather wet sandals are tied securely to the outside of his rucksack. James also makes sure Mick eats an energy bar and they all take swigs from their water bottles.

They stick closely to the path along the side of the lake and before long, they reach the head of the water and the path veers left into woodland before it climbs steadily through Ennerdale Forest. Eventually, they arrive at the Black Sail Hut. There are sounds of life coming from the inside, but apart from pausing for another drink and for Andy and Mick to take a quick bite from their provisions, they do not hang around. The sternest challenge of the day now lies ahead, as they have about a mile of steep climbing up the Black Sail Pass before a further two-and-a-half-mile descent to the Wasdale Head.

* * *

It is 5.30pm as they leave the apparent sanctuary of Black Sail Hut behind and start the long and twisting climb out of the valley. They can see the cliffs of the lower reaches of Kirk Fell above and to their left, whilst the Pillar Massif holds sway above and to the right.

"Last one to the top of the pass is a sissy," says Mick, in a fit of both bravado and to reassure the others he has regained his composure. He is still inwardly fuming at himself, both for going off-piste and for losing his sunglasses.

"We're still doing OK," says James, "I reckon we will still be at the pub by about 7.30pm."

"You can't exactly run up here," Andy points out.

He is not relishing the next forty minutes of

climbing, interspersed with one or two brief stops to catch his breath. Although he is the tallest and therefore has the longest legs of the three, the days when he could out stride his two compatriots up hills of this magnitude are long gone. Whilst he still does some jogging, he knows James and Mick are running more miles a week than he is now and, therefore, will have more strength.

Mick is pushing forward as the gradient steepens, and James isn't too far behind. Andy is resigned to taking as long as he needs to arrive at the high point with enough energy left to complete the descent to Wasdale Head (and to enjoy a pint when they get there).

They limit conversation as they slowly ascend the twisting track up the pass. Having a walking pole gives James the bonus of an extra 'limb' to lean on to pull himself up to some steeper parts. He knows it will be even more helpful to him on the descent to follow.

Mick's knee is throbbing, and it reminds him of both his stupidity and the challenge of being able to replace the sunglasses on a like-for-like basis, given how much they cost. Such thoughts take him back to wondering how things are at home and whether Louise is busy in the garden, or on the phone to either of the girls, worrying about how they are managing with the grandkids and whether they are having enough quality time.

Lost in such thoughts, he almost stumbles over a rock that rises higher than he thinks and as he regains his balance, realises that the high point of the pass is only a few metres away. He turns to survey the route they have taken and to check on the progress of James and Andy. James is about one hundred metres below him and has stopped to wait for Andy to catch up. He is leaning on his walking pole and taking a glug from his water bottle. Mick is suddenly aware of how fond he is of these two men, and of how straightforward conversation is with them both.

He sighs. "Not much further," he shouts, "I'm at the top!"

* * *

The descent to the Wasdale Head Inn takes longer than they think, but that seems to be the norm with the last part of any day's walk. It is 7.35pm when they get to the inn and collect the key to go up to their room. This has three beds and an en-suite bathroom with a shower. Last food orders are 8.30pm and this means they spent the next forty minutes getting showered and changed before they wearily trudge down the stairs to find the main bar area. It is packed with fellow hikers, bikers and locals.

A table is found, and the first pints are ordered whilst the menu is being scanned. They agree to order mains to be followed by a pudding. By the time the food arrives, the second pints are on the table and all three, whilst weary and relieved, can enjoy the evening. All are hungry. James is ravenous, and he shovels the food down as if to prove the point.

James is unaware of how fast he is eating, and he suddenly feels faint. The noise around seems to drift off into the distance. His head feels light and woolly, and he can't understand why he is so tired.

"I don't feel well," he murmurs. "Just want to rest my head."

He can hear Mick and Andy expressing their concerns and trying to get through to him. He is oscillating between the need to lie down and the need to be sick. Finally, he conveys the need for one or both of his friends to help him get to the toilets. They push unfinished plates of food to the side along with half-empty pints of beer as they extricate James from his collapsed state and half drag, half carry him to the toilet. They pass eyes showing a mixture of concern and contempt.

"Just leave me here," *to die*, he thinks, "I'll be alright in a moment or two."

Mick has gone back to the table, and he is reassuring other diners that his companion is OK, whilst Andy lingers a while to monitor James. The colour has drained from his face and he looks ashen. He was certainly a dead weight to manoeuvre to the toilets.

James, feeling slightly less faint and aware Andy is missing his dinner, insists he return to be with Mick.

"If I'm not with you in ten minutes, then come back to me, but I am feeling a little better."

Back at the table, Mick and Andy do a quick stock take on any known medical conditions James may have and draw a blank. Andy is googling the symptoms on his phone. It is Mick that points out he can't remember James having anything to eat—no snacks on any of the stops they had after their lunch at Ennerdale Bridge.

"He did rather dive into those Cumberland sausages," he adds.

"Well, according to what I can make out," says Andy, "the most likely thing that happened is all the blood rushed to his stomach to help with digesting the food he was shovelling in, and the blood must have drained from his head to deal with it."

"That would explain him feeling faint and keeling over."

Just then, a still ashen and wobbly James can be seen making his way carefully back to them, using every bit of furniture on route as a support.

"I'm feeling less faint," he says, "but if you don't mind, I think I'd like to go up to the room. I'm cold and shivery."

Neither Andy nor Mick have the appetite for more food or beer. They assist James out of the bar and climb the stairs to their room. James gets out of his clothes and slides under the covers, pulling the duvet right up to his neck. He feels cold, but at least the colour is returning to his face and he has stopped feeling nauseous.

"I didn't want a pudding anyway," says Mick, clearly intimating the highlight of his evening has been sorely missed.

"Or another pint," says Andy, "or even more scintillating conversation."

"I don't think we're going to get any scintillating conversation from him," says Mick, showing the prostrate James, who is already asleep.

"Until the morning then," says Andy, adding, "oh, how's the knee?"

"I'll live," says Mick, "which for a moment there, I wasn't sure whether we could say the same for James."

"It'll teach him not to eat his food so fast."
"Aye, a right greedy pig."
"Until the morning, then."
"Whatever that may bring."

CHAPTER THREE

James wakes first and is much better after his sleep. He knows immediately he was anything but alright last night, and is keen for his two companions to wake so he can apologise. But he doesn't want to compound his situation by waking either of them from their sleep. In the ten minutes before they rouse from their respective slumbers, he has plenty of time to revisit the events and the probable reasons for his collapse. He can also hear the rain pitter pattering on the windowpane and knows he will need to reconsider which route they should take today. Heading up onto Scafell Pike (before descending to Esk Hause and then continuing to the Langdale Valley across Esk Pike and Bow Fell) had been his preferred route. On a clear day that would be a splendid walk, but in mist and rain, it would be a more challenging one.

"Morning, James," says Mick, "how are you feeling?"

"A hell of a lot better than I did at the dinner table last night."

Andy is stirring and opens an eye before he speaks. "Morning. You feeling any better, James? What's the weather like?"

James confirms his improved demeanour to Andy and adds, "It was pouring earlier on, but it's turned into lighter rain at the moment, but you can't see over fifty metres in any direction."

"Doesn't sound like a shorts and sandals day then," says Mick.

"Er, no," says Andy.

James explains he has been contemplating the options for today's route and suggests climbing out of Wasdale to Sty Head may be the best option. They can then follow the path towards Esk Hause and the clear track down into the Langdale Valley.

"Let's discuss the options over breakfast," says Mick. "I'm feeling rather peckish. After all, I didn't get to eat any pudding last night."

"Good idea," says James, "whilst we can delay our departure a little, we must be away before 8am if we are to have any chance of catching our train home this evening."

As they make their way downstairs, James is ruminating; his original plan had been for them to set off by 7.30am as whichever route taken will probably require a good ten hours, factoring in any stops. Starting at 8am only allows for about half an hour leeway before the last train that will get them home this evening departs from Windermere. He is already feeling stressed at the prospect of a long day's walk in which he has to keep chivvying his friends to keep to their schedule.

It is already 7am. Mick can sense James's sense of frustration at the lack of urgency. He also knows were it not for his embarrassment about last night's collapse, he would push them more to get a move on. After yesterday's route march, he hoped for a gentler day today, but from James's comments, he realises the day will be another slog.

It is a morning for enjoying cooked breakfasts, with Andy, as usual, going for the 'veggie' option. They limit conversation when the food arrives. Before, they cover the events of yesterday, including James's collapse, today's route, and for Andy, reflections on how things might be at home with Melissa. James is anxious Sally doesn't know about his collapse last night.

"You won't mention my being unwell last night to Louise, will you? Don't want to risk Sally finding out."

"You're not the only one who can keep a secret," says Mick.

By the time they are all togged up and ready to go (breakfast having been well enjoyed and the bill paid), it is 8.15am and Andy and Mick can sense James is already stressing.

The advantage of a cooked breakfast is it provides a good load of carbs to keep you going and provides energy for the physicality of the task at hand. The disadvantage is starting any day by walking on a full stomach always slows you down at first. Today is no exception. The pull up and out of the Wasdale Valley to Sty Head, with the lower slopes of Great Gable to the left and the towering buttresses of the Scafell Massif on your right, is difficult at the best of times. With a full breakfast on board and a persistent light drizzle and swirling mists to contend with, progress is slow.

James is ahead, both to show he is feeling no ill effects from yesterday and to push the pace as much as he dares. The underfoot conditions aren't good, with any semblance of a path lost amongst the boulders, tufts of grass and sodden peaty moss randomly strewn under their feet. James is so intent on keeping going he plunges up to the knee in one particularly squelchy patch, having failed to test its stability first with his walking pole.

"Bollocks!" he explodes as he desperately tries to pivot on his grounded leg to extricate the submerged limb from the morass.

"More haste, less speed," is Mick's predictable response.

"Need a hand, James?" asks Andy, who is bringing up the rear.

He hadn't witnessed the manoeuvre that consumed half of his buddy's leg, but he was amused by the uncoordinated antics of his walking companion.

A chastened James takes a moment to remove as much of the gooey sludge from his trousers and walking boot, with the aid of his swiss army knife. Mick watches and remembers James never goes on any walk without it.

"I reckon that's the strangest use that knife's been put to yet," he says.

James smiles, but carries on with the task without responding.

Sticking closer together, the three eventually arrive at the top of Sty Head Pass and pause briefly to take stock, have a drink and work out their onward route. It has taken them an hour and three quarters to get here from the Wasdale Head Inn. James knows he has walked the same route in an hour and a quarter before and they are falling way behind their schedule if they are to catch their train home. As a backstop, he knows there will be bus and taxi options to get them the last four to five miles from Ambleside to Windermere if this proves necessary.

At the large cairn that marks the top of the pass, they bear right along a well-trodden and clear path that will take them to Esk Hause. The path periodically crosses little water courses as the run-off from the higher fells to their right, bisects their path, before plunging down to Sty Head Ghyll below. Andy remembers camping near there with his sister many years ago. They tickled a couple of trout in the Ghyll before gutting them and cooking them over a campfire for breakfast. Happy memories!

In later life, his sister turned increasingly to drink, and she has been a source of worry for Andy for some time. James's younger sister also suffered from anxiety and alcohol addiction and sadly passed away some five years ago, because of the latter. Andy often shares his concerns and experiences about his sister with James, who has been happy to advise and offer support based on his own experiences.

Andy is lost in such thoughts and again thankful that in James he has someone who he can both talk to and who understands the situation. Mick shakes him out of his introspection.

"Is that Great End to our right, peering occasionally out of the mist?"

"It most definitely is," says James, "remember our first visit to the summit, Mick?"

"I certainly do!"

It is a story Andy too is aware of, but he has never been in the incident's vicinity with his two walking friends before. In his forties James had climbed all the

2,000-foot peaks in the Lake District and in undertaking his self-imposed challenge concluded it would be apt to make the summit of Great End at 2,984 feet the last mountain to climb. Mick joined James on several of his excursions, as he gradually knocked off more and more of the Lakeland peaks.

It was in early May—Cup Final weekend in 1998— the pair had travelled up to Wasdale Head and climbed Great End. Whilst standing on the small summit plateau, a sudden gust of wind lifted James clean off his feet and took him backwards over the edge onto some rocks about fifteen feet below. His rucksack full of extra layers and food provisions cushioned him from any serious injury and, apart from being a little winded, he survived to tell the tale. Another two metres in either direction and the fall would have taken him much further down the mountain, led to serious injury, and potentially to his death.

James referred to the event as 'one of my nine lives' and Mick had never been so relieved, as he peered from the edge, which moments earlier James had 'sailed' over, to discover him lying like an upturned turtle, with a big grin on his face.

"Yes," he said. "That was definitely a great end."

As both their wives were awaiting their return in a cottage at Grange Over Sands and a celebratory meal and bottle of champers was on ice, Mick would certainly not have relished returning alone. His other abiding memory from that excursion was in each of the three pubs they called in on their journey back from Wasdale to Grange, none were showing the Cup Final.

***

The path zigzags through the mist, wide enough for a car to travel on, albeit so pitted and rocky and uneven even the most robust 4x4 would struggle to make progress. It climbs first left and then right before seeming to level out again. Mick is inwardly stressing about exactly where they are. They should have seen Sprinkling Tarn to their left by now. By his calculations, they should be nearer to the cross paths and shelter at Esk Hause, too. The mist makes visibility poor, but the tarn isn't far from the path, so why hasn't it been seen? He'd had one or two nightmare moments in Lakeland mists and been lost twice, once when Mick was with him.

Almost sensing his unease and his quietness, Mick suddenly says, "Not lost, are we, James?"

"No," says James, "not lost, but not exactly certain how far we've still to go to get to the cross path. I'll feel better when I've got a better handle on exactly where we are."

"Yes, always good to know exactly where you are!" says Andy.

"We're getting behind schedule, but unfortunately, you just can't make the same progress in these conditions. If it's any consolation, if we can get to Ambleside by 6.30pm, which we should still be able to do, we can catch a bus that will drop us off at Windermere Station with five minutes to spare before our train departs," says James.

"As long as five minutes? We've cut it finer than that before!" says Andy.

"Is that a crossroads of paths I see ahead?" says Mick.

A mightily relieved James confirms it appears to be. "There should be a large cairn to mark the spot and a shelter off to the right."

"There's certainly a large cairn," says Andy, as the shape and outline of the conical mound loom towards them from the mist.

"Keep straight on past the cairn and follow the path. It should start dropping to the left in about half a mile," says James.

A line of smaller cairns marks the path, each one ahead only visible just after the last one. Visibility is as bad as it has been since they left the Wasdale Head Inn two and a half hours ago. James knows their progress will remain slower than planned in such conditions and it will probably take them another three hours before they are at the Old Dungeon Ghyll at the head of the Langdale Valley. He hopes the valley will be mist-free and with minor roads and easy footpaths to follow, their onward progress from there should be good.

Andy's phone pings, and he stops to check it. The visibility is so poor James and Mick pause too, to ensure they remain in visual contact. Mick reminds James now might be a good time to have a snack and a drink of water.

"We don't want another episode like yesterday, do we?" he says.

James smiles sheepishly but agrees on a snack, even though he doesn't quite feel he's walked off the cooked breakfast yet. He delves into his rucksack to retrieve an oat bar and helps Mick off with his rucksack, so he can do the same.

"Bugger!"

"A message from Melissa?" says James.

"How did you guess? She can't find Millie's gym shoes and thinks I've hidden them somewhere and wonders why I'm never at home when I'm needed," Andy says. "I better respond. She sent the message about an hour ago and it's only just shown up. There's a signal here, but I'm not sure we'll have one for much longer. They'll probably be where they usually are, but if she's looked in the one place she thinks they should be, and they aren't there, she'll be getting into a strop about it."

Andy fires off a text. James helps Mick get his rucksack in place and tightens the straps and the three set off again into the mist, searching for the next cairn.

James is worried they haven't yet dropped to the left. They seem to climb slightly. He frantically scours the map and checks his compass to work out exactly where they are. Both Mick and Andy are used to James worrying about route finding. He is usually very good at it though, so his map studying is not thought to be of concern. After a few moments of walking slowly whilst consulting the map, James makes an announcement.

"Well, the good news is I've worked out exactly where we are. The not so good news is we are headed along a path that will take us up and over Esk Pike and Bow Fell and not on the planned route down Mickleden Beck. I don't quite know how we ended up on this path, but there are plenty of cairns to guide us."

After a few more steps, it is abundantly clear to them

all the path is rising with an increasing number of rocks to contend with. Suddenly, a figure looms out of the mist, heading for them, closely followed by a second. They are both clad in running gear, their mud-splattered legs testimony to the terrain they have traversed.

"Probably running the Bob Graham round," says Mick.

Their focus returns to ensuring they remain on the path, as it becomes less distinct amongst the rocks as they approach the higher reaches of Esk Pike. There are more and more bodies staggering out of the mist towards them. Shadowy, sinewy shapes braving the elements as they pick their way across the landscape; the first trusts luck and good judgement as he instantly memorises what he sees of the terrain ahead and runs blindly onwards. The rest are desperately trying to stay in touch with the runner directly in front to aid their progress through the murk. Once or twice, James, Mick and Andy quickly step aside to avert a headlong collision with an on-rusher, as another competitor appears. There are now female runners too, as the path falls away. The three have been so pre-occupied with avoiding the fell-runners they have missed the high point of Esk Pike and are now heading on towards Bow Fell.

On a clear day, Bow Fell is a magnificent vantage point from which to survey a plethora of other Lakeland summits and it provides a great 360-degree panorama of views, including the Irish sea to the south-west. Today visibility is ten metres and confined entirely to the Fell itself. The runners are now fewer and further apart and look increasingly desperate and at odds with their surroundings.

"You can almost hear their internal voices screaming out, 'what the hell am I doing here?', as our paths cross," says Andy.

"It must be a fell race of some description," says James. "You'd never see so many Bob Graham round runners in such a brief space of time."

James makes sure they all spot and visit the high point of Bow Fell before they start their descent into Borrowdale. There is a brief stop and another swig of water before they move on.

"No point having this inadvertent detour if we don't visit the summit," he says, as if to justify their slight deviation from the main footpath.

He and Mick had been up to Borrowdale earlier in the year and climbed up and down The Band to the summit of Bow Fell, and therefore James feels more confident of his route finding as they descend again. He is also abundantly clear they will now most definitely need to get a bus or taxi from Ambleside if they are to catch the train from Windermere. They may even have to summon a taxi from Skelwith Bridge if they fall any further behind schedule.

CHAPTER FOUR

As they descend and manoeuvre through the cascade of rocks and boulders randomly strewn across their path, James notices Mick now has only one sandal attached to the back of his rucksack. He is about to remark on this, but holds his breath half an instance.

Not before a 'Mick' has emerged from his lips, he recovers himself with, "Mi cagoule's really effective at keepin' out the wind!"

For the next thirty seconds, he undertakes the most extensive internal enquiry into the missing sandal. They can't afford any more unscheduled delays. He may have put it in his rucksack when they stopped at the summit. It may have come detached. It could be anywhere. He's bound to notice, eventually. Would it save more time to tell him now, or do they wait for the discovery? What is Mick's reaction going to be to the loss of a sandal, if it is indeed lost? Having weighed up all the options, he decides if it has come detached, it is most likely to be near the summit and if they stop now, it won't take more than five minutes to retrace steps there to locate it. He is about to draw Mick's attention to the sandal situation, when, much to his annoyance, Andy suddenly chimes in.

"I can only see one sandal hanging from your rucksack, Mick?"

"Bugger!" exclaims Mick, as he stops to take it off to see for himself.

45

"I was just about to point that out too," says James.

They conclude a quick discussion with an agreement Mick will retrace steps back up to the summit and scan around the area. They can all only remember the stop before when Andy needed to text Melissa about the gym shoes, and that is probably around a couple of miles back.

James asserts, "I'm sure there were two sandals in place on the way up to Bow Fell summit," as much to dissuade thoughts of any further backtracking. He hasn't a clue when he last saw both sandals.

Mick sets off (minus his backpack) through the morass of dark grey boulders looming out of the lighter grey of the swirling mist. Losing his sunglasses was bad enough, but to have to replace his favourite walking sandals too would warrant this trip being considered an unmitigated disaster. He is in a foul mood as he moves as quickly as he can, scanning the ground for a missing sandal.

Meanwhile, Andy and James take stock of where they are and of the rest of today's route.

James accepts, "Once we have found the main descent path down 'The Band', route finding should be plain sailing."

Langdale is a favourite area of Andy's and he is looking forward to being able to traverse the smaller lanes and lower-level footpaths that lie ahead. He can sense James's anxiety at the impact, yet another unscheduled delay may have on getting to Windermere on time.

"Look," he says, "we both know there is a wonderful cafe and gift shop at Skelwith Bridge, and what better place to wait awhile for a taxi to arrive to take us to Windermere, if that's what we have to do?"

Out of the mist a familiar figure emerges, bearing down on them with greater alacrity than the underfoot conditions should allow. The picture of Mick with a huge smile on his face clutching a sandal, which he holds aloft like some hard-won trophy, is one that will live in the memories of both James and Andy for many a year to come.

"I bloody found it," he says, "just below the summit cairn. Can you believe it?"

"I'm so glad we both noticed it was missing when we did," says James, secretly wishing he'd spoken thirty seconds earlier.

* * *

Rucksacks are reacquainted with backs, and straps are adjusted. The three of them set off again in search of the broad and steep descent into Borrowdale. As they do so, the last of the fell runners—more heavily built than those who have gone before and at least twenty minutes behind his predecessor—slowly makes his way past them. They all wish him well and confirm he is less than two minutes away from the summit of Bow Fell.

"I'm glad I'm not in his shoes," says Mick as soon as he is out of earshot.

"Or sandals," says Andy.

It is not long before James is recognising familiar stretches of the path as it descends the fell into the valley below. He remembers sections of the route for the next mile or so are paved or stepped to prevent the continual erosion of the existing path. Less stressed, he has accepted even walking to Ambleside to catch a bus or taxi to Windermere is going to be pushing it now. Andy's comments have given him a realistic perspective. Getting to Skelwith Bridge alone will have made today's route a testing, yet enjoyable walk. They can always return and continue their journey across northern England, in the next section of their walk.

As the land falls away and the descent gets deeper into the valley, the mists thins and they can see fleeting glimpses of greener pastures below.

Andy, unlike James, is inwardly dreading the descent down the Fell because he hates going downhill. He must shorten his stride pattern and be more deliberate at placing his feet. He admires the way James almost seems to speed up on a descent and the confidence he has in his sense of balance, using his lower point of equilibrium.

It also impresses him how James uses his walking pole in his manoeuvres. *Maybe I should invest in a walking pole?* he thinks. Andy's internal question has been asked a few times of late. He has resisted before now, feeling walking poles, for him, are a concession to the ageing process and one he isn't yet ready to take.

"The mists are clearing. The sun is coming out!" shouts James.

He stands astride the path, waiting for both Andy and Mick to reach him. Within a few seconds, they are looking down and along the whole swathe of the Langdale valley, with its patchwork of walled fields, meandering minor roads and tracks with the grey-white specks of sheep dotted amongst the greens. The silvery thread of Great Langdale Beck winds into the distance. At the farm at the base of the Fell, they can see a field of parked cars glistening in the sun and a marquee too.

"That must be where the race started from," says Andy.

"Only a mile beyond is the Old Dungeon Ghyll," says James. "Andy and I were discussing the rest of the walk whilst you were retrieving your lost sandal. Realistically, even getting to Ambleside in time to get a taxi or bus to Windermere Station might push it now, so we hatched a plan C, which would mean catching a bus or taxi from Skelwith Bridge. It's about five or six miles from the ODG to Skelwith Bridge, so even with our lunch stop we should get there by 4.30pm."

"Talking of lunch," says Andy, "I'm feeling a little peckish. Now we are walking in the sun, should we find a suitable spot to stop on the way down?"

"We can either do that or wait till we get to the Old Dungeon Ghyll," says James. "We can always wash it down with a pint."

"We'll take stock and reconsider the options in half an hour," says Mick.

They set off again with James in front, followed by Mick and Andy, the latter still inwardly stressing about the descent. *I'll just take my time,* he says to himself, as he eases his way down another steep step and then twists first left and then right as the direction of the flagstones and slabs dictates. He takes his mind off the apprehension of the job by letting his mind wander to his children and what they will be doing at home. Just as the image of Millie reading from The Prisoner of

Azkaban solidifies in his head, Andy's feet go completely from under him, and he falls. Instinct takes over and he reaches down to prevent continuing any further forward. His hands and wrists take the full impact. He is immediately aware of the searing pain in his left wrist.

"Aaagh!" He lets out an audible gasp of pain.

James is too far below to hear, but Mick turns immediately to witness the slumped form of Andy, sprawled across the path.

"Are you ok, Andy?" asks Mick.

"Rather shocked, and I've jolted or damaged my wrist, I think. I'll just take a few moments to recover my composure."

Mick shouts down to James that Andy has fallen, and he turns around to look back up the fell side. He can see Andy sitting on the path about ten metres above, where the slabs and pavers give way to an earth track. It marks the last section of their descent. He can also see Mick climbing back up to where Andy is.

Andy is ashen when Mick reaches him and shaken by the fall. There is blood and grazing on and around both his hands, but it is clearly the left wrist that is causing most concern.

"I think I may have just jarred it," he says, pointing to the wrist. Inwardly, he feels the injury may be more serious, as the pain is excruciating and making him feel a little nauseous.

"Just take some time," says Mick. He helps Andy off with his rucksack and retrieves some water.

Below, James has stopped, and he takes off his rucksack and delves into the depths to retrieve the first aid kit. He'd packed it on Thursday night without fully checking the contents and he needs to appraise himself of what is in it before offering anything useful. He finds a gauze bandage, some Ibuprofen gel, and thankfully a couple of antiseptic wipes and plasters. For a moment, he thinks all such items may have been used yesterday when administering first aid to Mick.

"Shall I come up?"

"Good idea," shouts Mick.

As James arrives on the scene, Andy, whilst still in pain, is feeling a little less shaken and asks James and Mick to help him to his feet. James uses the wipes to gently clean away the dirt and grit from Andy's hands. Grazes on both are visible, but there doesn't appear to be a need to apply any plasters. There is swelling around the left wrist and James rigs up a makeshift sling with the gauze.

"I've got a thin pair of gloves, Andy. You could wear one on your right hand and borrow my walking pole to provide extra support. The glove will prevent any chafing from gripping."

"That might be helpful," agrees Andy.

"Bloody ironic you were almost at the end of the slabbed steps when you slipped," says Mick, "because another few feet and you'd have been rid of them. There should be a first aider and maybe a more extensive kit at Stool End Farm, where the fell runners started from. I can see one or two people milling around."

The three of them set off again with Andy walking gingerly, albeit it is now much easier going on the earth track. James and Mick take it in turns to carry Andy's rucksack and their own. It takes about another ten minutes to get to the farm and Mick goes off to find someone who may provide a more stable sling, administer some pain relief, and give Andy a bit of a once over.

He returns to where James and Andy are waiting with a face like thunder.

"Apparently there is no dedicated first-aider on hand and whilst the people I saw think there may be a kit somewhere, neither has any idea where it is. I'm damn sure you shouldn't be organising a fell race without having such provisions in place!" he adds.

Mick used to be a health and safety officer before taking up a more general human resources role.

"Only about another twenty minutes and we'll be at the Old Dungeon Ghyll," says James. "We may get further help there."

"Aye, and have that spot of lunch we promised ourselves about an hour ago," says Mick.

At the Old Dungeon Ghyll, they can sit outside on one of the many picnic tables. Most are occupied with other walkers, day trippers and families, all basking in the warm sun. Mick goes inside to order some drinks— a weak tea with milk and sugar for Andy, rather than a pint. He is still in considerable pain and believes it must either be a bad sprain or a break. He curses his stupidity at losing concentration and, as a result, his footing.

James has also reached a similar conclusion about his friend's wrist and is already surmising Melissa will delight in clarifying James is at fault, as he should not be organising such demanding walking challenges.

"The three of you are not spring chickens anymore," he can hear her saying.

James rubs more Ibuprofen gel onto the affected area of Andy's wrist and takes time to rig up a more supportive sling. Mick returns with the round of drinks and the three finally tuck into their packed lunches.

Over lunch, they discuss what the most sensible option is. It is half-past two and they would do well to even make Skelwith Bridge by 5pm. James is still inwardly dreading what Melissa's reaction to Andy's injury will be and feels he should do the sensible thing and bring this leg of their journey to a premature close.

"I'll see if they've got the number for a local taxi firm behind the bar," he says. "The chances are we could catch an earlier train and ensure we get home that bit earlier too."

"Good idea," says Mick.

Andy thinks about protesting as he knows how much James was looking forward to today's walk. He would, on another day, have really enjoyed the next section of the walk, through Chapel Stile and Elterwater. The pain in his wrist though is showing no sign of abating, and he accepts getting home sooner is an appealing prospect.

* * *

It takes a further thirty minutes before the taxi arrives, which is mirrored by the time taken to deliver them to the concourse of Windermere Station. They have a fifteen-minute wait for a train and have changes to make at Carnforth and Skipton. Andy considers ringing

Melissa to cadge a lift from Skipton, but decides discretion is the better part of valour and a bus from Shipley will get him home by six thirty, two hours early. He hopes his premature return will go some way to enabling Melissa to be in a positive mood and for her to take on sympathy.

Mick is debating when to telephone Louise and inform her of his early return, Andy's potentially broken wrist, and the need for a lift from Shipley station. He makes the call after they join the Carnforth to Skipton train.

It is abundantly clear from Mick's comments Louise's response to the phone call is exactly as James imagined it would be. There is, however, enough concern about Andy for her to readily agree to pick him up from Shipley.

"Can you also drop James off at home too?" he hears Mick ask.

As the call ends, he turns to James and Andy and confirms Louise has volunteered to drop them both at home.

That could be an interesting experience, thinks Andy. "Thanks for that, Mick," he says.

James wants to ask about agreeing dates for the next leg of their coast-to-coast journey, but wonders whether there will ever be another section to the walk, given the events of the last two days.

At Shipley, Louise is waiting outside the station in the car as James and Andy, both feeling somewhat sheepish, emerge with Mick. He loads their rucksacks in the boot before opening the rear passenger doors for his friends.

"Well?" she says. "What the hell were you doing coming down Bow Fell? I didn't realise you intended to be walking that route. Didn't you and James climb up and down it a couple of months ago?"

Fair play to Mick, he doesn't say, 'We didn't intend to be on that path, but James missed the right path in the mist at Esk Hause and we ended up going over Esk Pike and Bow Fell by mistake.' Instead, he says, "Andy's feet went from under him and instinct took over."

"We better get him home for Melissa to administer some TLC," is her response.

They spend the rest of the journey in silence until Andy is dropped off at home.

CHAPTER FIVE

It was the following spring before the next leg of the challenge got underway. November and December saw heavy rains lash the north of England, and parts of Cumbria experienced significant flooding. Evidence of the impact had been visible from the train virtually all the way from Gargrave to Kendal. Sunshine was the order of the day though, as they strolled out of the station and sought the taxi Andy summoned prior to their arrival.

James was inwardly grimacing at the late change in plans. Initially, it had been hard enough for him to accept today's walk would start from Windermere, rather than involve backtracking to the Old Dungeon Ghyll. He then had to compromise further and accept they would start at Staveley, because Mick insisted.

"We've walked from Windermere to Staveley before."

He sourced a train to drop them off at Staveley, but that would have got them there for eleven. Getting the earlier train to Kendal and getting a taxi to Staveley meant they could begin by ten thirty.

"That will give us half an hour more to enjoy the evening in Sedbergh," Andy reasoned.

For Andy, today's new itinerary attracted pragmatism. Whilst Melissa's views about continuing this 'crazy adventure' mellowed over the months, she had been clear to Andy when she said, "Staveley to

Sedbergh was quite far enough for a man still recuperating from a broken wrist!"

He winced at remembering her words (and the pointed delivery of them) and his fall from grace on Bow Fell. He had gone to A and E at Airedale Hospital on the Monday after their return and received confirmation his wrist was fractured. It took the best part of three months before the NHS was happy enough with his recovery and a further two months before Melissa agreed a discussion about continuing the walk could be arranged. Andy even got himself a walking pole and has been on a couple of half day walks recently to get comfortable using it. It still feels rather strange; although it has helped to restore his confidence on the downhill stretches he has practised on.

Mick, resplendent in a new pair of shorts, sandals and a jazzy pair of sunglasses (with blue rims that seem to attract and then reflect light in a myriad of colour flashes) is pleased to be back with his two walking buddies. From what he understands, today will see them walking a splendid section of the Dales Way, albeit in reverse. The Dales Way was a journey the three shared about ten years ago, and he had fond memories.

As the taxi approach Staveley, their driver asks, "Which side of the village do you want me to drop you in? They haven't fully repaired the bridge in the middle since the December floods swept part of it away."

"This side would be best," says James. "We're going to be walking south-eastwards to Sedbergh."

"You could drop us past the level crossing," says

Andy, "and we can pick up our route from there, can't we?"

He addresses the latter comment to James, rather than to the taxi driver, who is pleased he will simply have to do a U-turn in the road, rather than a three-point once the southern approach to the stricken bridge is reached.

They bundle out of the taxi, pay the fare, and lift rucksacks onto shoulders before both Mick and Andy wait on James's instructions before moving off. James has been secretly hoping to visit the bridge to survey the damage. He also can't quite remember which side of the river the Eagle and Child Inn are on. They have all enjoyed previous stop-overs there, and he hopes it hasn't suffered flood damage. He knows at this time of day the pub won't be open, so a visit to its vicinity will not lead to a delayed start. His wistful gaze must convey what is in his mind.

Mick says, "I think you'll find we need to head this way, James. That way leads to the Eagle and Child."

"Yes, I know," says James. "I was just wondering whether our favourite pub had escaped the flooding. It was right next to the bridge as I remember it."

"Just this side of it," says Andy. "Do you remember the first time we stayed there?"

They had been sitting at a table in the dining area for about twenty minutes, expecting someone to come and take their food order. It was only when Mick went to order another round of drinks and complained about their wait that they informed him food needed to be ordered at the bar. They all laugh as they remember their foolishness.

"Right then," says James, "let's get this leg of the walk underway. If we wait any longer, we might as well have got the later train and saved on the taxi."

* * *

It isn't long before the three are walking alongside the river Kent—glistening and babbling waters flowing gently, catching and reflecting the spring sunshine as they pass by. About fifty metres beyond their path and higher up the gentle slopes of the fields they are walking through are curving lines of debris, driftwood and vegetation, demonstrating how far and wide the river was about four months ago. There is also ample evidence of entire trees or large branches, broken off in their prime and now strewn across fields they'd stood beside for many years. Once or twice, the usual path is left to avoid such debris.

At one of these obstacles, Andy tries to lift both legs and his walking pole over and across a gnarled lump of a tree. Right foot, walking pole and fallen tree come together and James and Mick watch aghast as he affects a rather dramatic and astonishingly balletic pirouette, before he tumbles head over heels onto the grass.

"You alright, Andy?" they ask in unison.

"No harm done," says Andy, getting back to his feet with a rueful look back at the tree. "Not quite got the hang of this stick yet."

He brandishes the offending walking pole as if it is a magician's wand. They emerge from the riverbank and walk through and beside the Cowan Head Luxury apartments, created within the structure of a former mill.

"Are you sure you don't need me to find you a luxury apartment all on one level, sooner rather than later?" quips Mick.

He has been telling James about a visit to see the grandchildren with Louise, feeling blessed and at one with the world. After another short stretch by the river, the three must find their way round the Handsome Brewery, with the smell of malt and hops hanging in the air. Another short stretch across fields brings them to a large paper mill complex, and the route does several doglegs as it skirts the mill buildings. They are now walking beside the River Sprint as it dashes southwards on a journey of confluence with the much larger River Lune.

Mick's phone suddenly pings, and he stops to consider the message. It is usually Andy who has contact from Melissa to contend with on their walks. The message is from Louise, checking all is well and he and Andy haven't been hoodwinked into walking further than planned. Mick carefully chooses the words he uses in response; it will have to be short, but sufficiently informative to allay any concerns and to convince her the Mountain Rescue number she has committed to memory will not be needed.

"Beautiful walk by the river. Sun is shining, and we can take in the scenery. Making good progress. Ring you tonight. Love, Mick." This gets nods of approval from both James and Andy before he hits send.

They arrive at the busy A6 and James consults his map before guiding them left to look out for a sign to the right in about two hundred metres. It is a relief when Garnett Folds Lane appears, and they can stop playing 'dodge the car' and enjoy an exhilarating short pull uphill before they spot a bench at the top of the rise. There is a view across rolling hills to the south.

"Good place for a lunch-stop," says Andy.

"I'll second that."

Mick is already slackening the straps on his rucksack, ready to offload and delve inside for his packed lunch. There is just enough room for the three to sit side-by-side on the bench.

"We've made good progress," says James.

Andy lays his walking pole next to James's, as he has on each of their stops during the morning to date. "That way I won't forget it."

The sun has temporarily gone behind a cloud and without it, the temperature feels more like February than April.

Another 'ping' sees Mick and Andy reach to their pockets. This time it is Andy and not Mick who has a message. Melissa has locked Millie and herself out of the house. Her parents have a spare key but live about twelve miles away, and she is wondering whether Andy has left a spare key with anyone nearer to home.

Why would I? he thinks. You don't just dole duplicates of your house keys out willie-nilly!

He decides the situation requires a phone call rather than a text message. Whilst he remembers his sister may have a spare key, she lives virtually the same distance away from Otley. Melissa doesn't take too kindly to this alternative suggestion and suddenly it is all his fault she is locked out. If he were not gallivanting half-way across the world, she'd be able to be back inside in no time at all. Andy blames himself and feels inadequate—it is an all too familiar pattern, and he suddenly feels all the positivity ebbing away faster than the waters of the River Sprint.

Both James and Mick sense the change in Andy's demeanour after the phone call and seek to lift his spirits. In the sun's absence, even the sunglasses he is wearing (to rival Mick's) seem to have lost their colourful swagger.

"It'll only take her an hour to get her hands on a spare set of keys and be back in the house," he says. "I should have made sure she knew where the spares are. I know worse things happen at sea, but I feel it's all my fault." In his head, he is imagining if Melissa wants to make a drama out of the incident, there is no one better qualified to do so.

Their route now takes them further along Garnett Folds Lane until they are back onto a path crossing open fields and skirting the edge of Black Moss Tarn. Here, James realises Andy no longer has his walking pole. Andy, distracted by the phone call, is oblivious to its absence. James curses his inability to take care of both walking poles and immediately points out the absence of Andy's stick and his responsibility. Fearing what they might say if Andy returns home minus the pole, he suggests they take a breather where they are so he can run back to their resting place to retrieve it. Andy is still reeling from the impact of his phone call to offer any protest and Mick sheepishly accepts Andy shouldn't return without it.

Before any further debate about the matter can take

place, James (minus his rucksack) is running as fast as he can back toward Garnett Folds Lane. He takes less than five minutes to cover the half mile to the bench, where the pole is lying next to the end of the seat Andy had been sitting at. Scooping it up, James makes his way once again along the lane.

In James's absence, Mick is once again offering Andy support and advice about how to stop blaming himself for every little thing that goes wrong. He is sure Melissa doesn't want him to, and the phone call was a natural response to try to find a solution to being locked out. He shouldn't let the call derail for him the clear improvements, over the past months, in his self-confidence. Andy assumes because Melissa is ten years his junior, she will tire of him and want a man of her own age at some point.

"Has she ever given you cause to think like that?" asks Mick.

"Well, no, but it's only a matter of time."

"That's not true, she thinks the world of you."

By the time James returns with the misplaced pole, Andy, thanks to Mick, is feeling less stressed. James is relieved they have averted a potential future excuse to limit their adventures.

"Right then, onwards and upwards."

* * *

The land rises to breast a low ridge ahead as they leave the Tarn behind and then cross the River Mint at Thursgill Beck. A right and then a left at the A685 takes them over Lambrigg Beck and they can both hear and see the M6 motorway ahead. They walk alongside a fence, beyond which the main west coast rail route between Glasgow and London runs, before arriving at Challon Hall farm. Beyond that, the road bridges over the motorway.

It is a Friday afternoon, and the motorway is busy with vehicles rushing below their feet. The M6 is one of the most significant fault lines they need to cross on their route across the breadth of the north of England.

CHAPTER SIX

At the T-junction beyond the motorway, they pick up the Dales Way route by going left, along the Old Scotch Road. This road not only pre-dates the motorway but was in common use prior to the construction of the A6.

"Is there another way we can get to Sedbergh, without continuing on the Dales Way?" asks Andy. "I do like the route, but we have walked it before, and I fancy a bit of a change of scenery."

Mick inwardly freezes. He is used to James throwing in the odd curve ball during a walk, but it isn't something he expects from Andy. He knows if there is a way, James will leap at the chance to identify it and then delight in navigating them. Such deviations haven't always had a successful or stress-free outcome. Mick also knows if they both agree to follow an alternative route, he will agree.

He can hear Louise's voice in his head, "Well! You and Andy didn't have to go along with it, did you? Stand up for yourself, the pair of you. Common sense should prevail."

James has already got the map spread out in his hand and is tracing fingers along it, with a look of meaningful concentration on his face.

"Well," he says, "if we go to the right and then take a left turn, we will walk along narrow single-track roads for a couple of miles, and then at a farm we can bear left and drop to go through a wood and re-join the Dales Way where it joins the A683."

"Sounds OK," says Andy.

"Not very exciting though," says Mick.

"Ah well, there is a particular feature we must pass which you may find very interesting," adds James, keeping the identity of, 'whatever it is' a closely guarded secret.

"Let's go for it," says Andy.

Mick is silent and bears his resignation to the changes with stoicism. He now has another quandary to consider. If the 'whatever it is' is indeed worth the detour, does this get mentioned to Louise when asked about the walk? For to do so will risk letting her know they deviated from the planned route. He could suggest it was a well-marked shortcut and got them to Sedbergh slightly earlier than otherwise would have been the case. Knowing how such route deviations have manifested in the past, though, his fears are more that it will take more time to get to their evening resting place instead.

James and Andy have already surged ahead, as if the changed route has given them new impetus. They are already at the junction that will see them leave the Old Scotch Road.

"You alright, Mick? We need to turn left here," says James.

"Just working on my script for Louise, if this brief detour of yours comes up," says Mick as he strides towards them. They all laugh.

The remark reminds James how much he enjoys the company of Mick. He is a great friend, and they have shared many a story of how to best manage their respective 'life partnerships'. He recognises Mick may indeed have to explain to Louise the rationale for the change in their route.

"You can always tell her it was a shortcut," he suggests.

"Yes, I've clocked that one," replies a smiling Mick.

They are now walking along Shacklabank Lane, which at first twists and winds its way uphill, before levelling out and then seems to drop as far as the eye can see.

"Look," says James, "you can see Sedbergh in the distance."

Mick concedes it does look like their evening resting place, about five miles ahead, is in sight.

"Splendid long-distance views anyway," says Andy.

He is still ruminating on his response to the conversation with Melissa. It is about an hour since the phone call and he bites the bullet and texts her to make sure she has picked up some keys and is back in the house.

Walking along the road isn't Mick's favoured walking option, but at least they won't get lost and the scenery is pleasant. The three have walked about a third of the way down the lane from its high point and are walking towards a small stand of old trees ahead. James is already expecting what they will shortly see and is about to announce to the others what lies ahead. However, before he can continue and lead them to the major point of interest, the familiar ping of Andy's phone causes them all to stop and hold their breath.

"She's gained entry and is apologising for bothering me in the first place," he says, grinning.

The smile is infectious and spreads across the faces of Mick and James.

"You can relax again," says Mick, "and enjoy the whatever it is James is hopefully going to show us soon."

There is slight irritation in his voice, as he believes the whole thing was a ruse from James to get them to go a different way.

A small graveyard appears on their left. Stone walls bound it and has trees are planted within it. They have been bent and shaped by the wind.

"This isn't the 'whatever it is'?" Mick wants to know.

"Partly," says James, "but the more interesting bit should be further on amongst some rocks to our left. There are a few headstones in evidence, but most are laid flat. This is one of the first Quaker burial grounds ever created. Apparently, there was a small chapel here to begin with, but that was destroyed in a storm in 1839 and subsequently rebuilt on the other side of the Fell."

James heads along a little footpath that takes them into an area where several large rocks create a miniature mountainous landscape. He scans the rocks and, with a keen eye, leads them to a prominent outcrop.

"Here we are," he says. "This is the spot where George Fox addressed over a thousand people in a sermon lasting three hours in June 1652. It was probably the occasion that gave rise to the birth of the

Quaker movement, hence the subsequent creation of the graveyard."

"It was probably heady stuff on that day," says Mick.

"Few current orators could hold an audience of a thousand for three hours," says Andy.

"It was shortly after the Civil War and few people were overly enamoured with the established church. Charles the first had been beheaded, Scotland had been invaded and was under English military rule, and the area around here was crying out for a way forward that represented ordinary people more effectively," says James.

"Get you, mister encyclopaedia Britannica," says Andy. "I bet you can tell us what size shoes Fox was wearing too!"

"Size six," is James's immediate response. "Only joking!" He laughs. "And there's no need for sarcasm. I've been here once before and remember some details of the time. We did that period in history when I was at school. Some things just stick."

"Talking of sticks," says Mick, "don't leave that there."

He gestures at Andy's walking pole, which is propped up against the rock next to the plaque which commemorates the George Fox sermon. Andy was about to walk away without it again.

Andy smiles and turns to pick up the pole before the three of them head back to the road.

"An interesting minor detour, James," Mick says. "I'm sure it will impress Louise."

* * *

James is feeling well appreciated and wonders whether now's the time to mention once they get to Shacklabank Farm, their route is along a footpath, which seems to disappear on the map, before the wood they must go through. There is a track on the map which connects the far side of the wood and appears to drop to the road. He decides not to throw any dampener on the current high spirits and trusts all will be well.

It is probably a further mile before the Farm is reached and James indicates the footpath sign that will take them off the road and across fields, where sheep and lambs are happily enjoying the Spring sunshine. They head along the track, which peters out as they enter the third field.

"Just head in the direction the arrow was pointing," suggests a confident James.

After a while, this seems to take them straight into the line of an unbroken stone wall. Further left and up a steep bank is a rocky outcrop, with the tops of trees just visible to its right.

"I think we need to head up there," says a suddenly less confident James.

"Not lost again are we?" asks Mick.

"No, the route takes us through a wood, and I can see the outline of the start of it just beyond those rocks," says James.

Arriving at the rock face, the three then edge around it whilst trying to balance on ground sloping at a forty-five-degree angle. Once they have circumnavigated the rocks, they can see the wood lies in front of them about a hundred metres away.

Confidence returns for Mick. Maybe James is following something other than an imaginary route? This doesn't last long though, for the wood is bounded by a barbed wire fence and there is no obvious way into it. To the left and at the top of the line of trees, a stone wall runs down to meet the wood. Where the wall and wood meet, it seems to be in a state of semi-collapse.

"Up there," James says and points, as if there is a clearly marked footpath leading to the spot.

"Are you sure?" asks Andy

"No, but I can't see any other way to go. If we can get into the field beyond the wall, we can walk down it until we find an easier way to get into the wood," says a far from confident James.

At the apex of wall and wood, as well as the tumble of fallen stones, another barbed wire fence bars their way. Several very rickety and rotten wooden posts support it. However, this arrangement means if one of them pushes down on a post, the barbed wire can lower to a height that facilitates crossing. Having worked this out, James volunteers to negotiate the obstacle first. Mick pushes down on the post and whilst this lowers the wire to a height of around two feet, a second line of barbed wire suddenly rises to a similar height and now presents a further obstacle. James must step over and between the two lengths of wire before he can clear the second one. This manoeuvre takes place whilst planting feet on an unstable platform of fallen stones.

Having watched James successfully reach the field

beyond the wall, Andy now tries to repeat the operation. As he raises a leg to cross the second wire, stones beneath his foot slide away and he is suddenly falling forward onto the barbed wire. Instinctively, he turns and tries to roll the obstacle, which luckily results in no part of his body being in contact with the rusty wire. However, a pocket of his anorak doesn't escape so lightly, and he now has a small, jagged tell-tale tear in the garment.

"Bloody buggar!" he exclaims. "It's Melissa's waterproof jacket. She'll go ballistic. I wouldn't mind, but it's the most expensive bit of walking kit she's ever bought and she hardly ever wears it. I feel honour bound to use it to justify the cost." He bemoans this sudden reversal of his fortunes and, for the rest of the walk into Sedbergh, is in a foul mood.

The other problem they now face is how to get Mick across. He can hardly hold the post down at the same time as seeking to clamber to where James and Andy are now standing. Eventually, they work out Mick will have to duck under the original barbed wire line whilst ensuring he doesn't snag himself on either of them. Rucksacks and walking poles are passed and thrown across and Mick steadies himself before successfully gaining firmer ground beside them. James aids his crossing by lifting the first line of barbed wire a little higher with the aid of his outstretched walking pole.

The three of them take stock and have a bite to eat and a drink from water bottles. Whilst they are doing this, James wanders down the line of the wall, returning with the good news there is somewhere lower down where they should be able to cross into the wood.

There is also the not so good news: the crossing will have a length of barbed wire to stride over too.

It has taken them an hour to cover the last mile and any thoughts this may be a shortcut have long since faded. Once in the wood, they make better progress. There are many clumps of bluebells yet to burst forth into bloom.

"This would be an excellent place to visit in about a month's time," says James.

"You'll be on your own then," says Mick, wanting to put this entire experience way behind them.

A path suddenly appears, and they follow it to a stile by a corner of the wood and it then drops to a further stile into a field. They can now see the main A683 road just ahead and join it for a short while before a Dales Way sign beckons them to cross into another field and drop down to walk beside the river again. They are now walking beside the River Rawthey and follow it all the way to the outskirts of Sedbergh, before they leave nature behind and head up into the town.

* * *

They have two rooms booked in a small guest house and are relieved to make its acquaintance. James and Mick will share a twin room and Andy will have a room for himself. The host welcomes them, shows them to their rooms, gives pointers for where to dine later, and instructs them to fill in forms with their breakfast requests before they go out. It is just 6pm by the time their host leaves them alone, with the breakfast order requirement still ringing in their ears.

They agree to congregate at 7pm and head into the town to the recommended restaurant, with the promise of fine dining to look forward to. To be fair, it doesn't disappoint. The puddings are spectacular. Add a few beers and a glass of wine to the mix, and even Andy has mellowed again by the time they are ready to leave and return to the guesthouse, knowing full well what each will have for their breakfast, in the morning.

CHAPTER SEVEN

The day dawns bright and breakfast, though predictable, is enjoyable, with Andy particularly enjoying the vegetarian option. They are out of the door and thanking the primary host at precisely 9am and are all looking forward to a walk that will be an unfamiliar experience for them all, apart from James. Even he has only walked the last bit of it from Ravenstonedale to Kirkby Stephen before. A quick stock up with a few additional provisions in the town, before heading north eastwards out and along the lower slopes of the Howgills. The route takes them along narrow lanes, to and between farmsteads and on footpaths through fields and by hedgerows, over water courses and stiles and through gates; each seeming to have its own way of being opened.

All three are wearing shorts. Andy has his sun hat firmly in place and strangely, Mick is wearing his sunglasses over his eyes and not perched on his head, where they usually sit.

James has worked out a route to Kirkby Stephen, following footpaths clearly marked on the OS map he has in his map-case. He doesn't intend for them to leave the planned route during the day's walk. There is a train at 4.10pm from the station at Kirkby Stephen. Even allowing an hour for stops along the way, they should easily make the station by 4pm. He has spoken to his wife Sally, and she has suggested there is an invisible tape that can be ironed to the inside of the torn cagoule pocket. If this is done carefully, the tear will be virtually unseen from the outside. He shared this information with Andy over breakfast. Sally has even offered to undertake the repair herself if Andy is prepared to let her have the garment for a day or two.

"Given the infrequent occasions when she wears the damn thing, she'll probably never spot the repair anyway," he suggests to his friend.

Andy is happier knowing there may be a way in which the rip in the cagoule may never need to be mentioned. He had a further positive message from Melissa last night, in which she said she was looking forward to seeing him this evening and offering to pick him up from the station if that would be helpful.

The warmth of the sun helps their moods and as they go through the fifth gate of the morning, they encounter their third jogger running towards them in a bright pink short-sleeve top and a pair of lime green and two-tone blue slacks, blonde hair held in place with a matching headband.

"Morning, lovely day for it," they chime in virtual unison as they hold the gate open for her to pass.

"Morning." She beams a smile of contentment, at one with herself.

"I'd probably be out with the Harriers this morning if I wasn't here with you two," says James.

"Yes, I'd be out running too," says Mick.

"I might be out running," says Andy, "but then again, probably not."

"This section of the walk is a delight, isn't it?" says

Mick. "Gentle climbs, meandering paths, interesting buildings and working farms."

"And a brilliant view across the valley to our right," says James.

"And the recumbent sleeping elephants of the Howgills on our left," adds Mick.

"Recumbent sleeping elephants!" exclaims Andy.

"Mick's right, that's how they are often referred to. Have a look at them next time you're driving between Kendal and Shap on the M6."

They continue to alternate between walking on narrow lanes that link and interconnect the occasional houses and farms they are passing through to the valley below, and footpaths across fields, beside streams and through copses. A steeper climb takes them alongside the edge of an escarpment with a watercourse down below to their left. They go over the shoulder of a hill before dropping to a gap in a stone wall, where the watercourse and footpath come together. A metalled road rises steeply from the gap in the wall. In the dip, the land is flatter, and the watercourse has expanded to create larger pools of water that will need to be crossed to access the road itself. The water is tumbling down the hillside to join and widen these pools, before slipping gently over the brim of a ledge, before rushing down along the bed it has carved in the belly of the hillside they climbed.

"Mmm," says Mick, "this could be tricky."

James and Andy watch as he carefully picks his way across, trying to judge which rocks may be stable enough to put a foot on and which may protrude above the water, or at least not lie more than an inch below it.

He takes a couple of minutes, but eventually, he is back on terra firma.

"Just take your time and select the right rocks to stand on and you'll be fine," he says.

"After you," says Andy, "you'll be quicker than me."

James observes Mick's route well, and he takes about thirty seconds to join him on the tarmac road.

Andy is inwardly dreading crossing the ford. Part of him wants to stride across and not worry too much about getting wet feet, but he only has his lighter weight walking shoes on and there are still six hours walking ahead. He has his walking pole to test the depth of the water in the different pools. He steps onto the first stone both his friends used and then carefully onto the second rock. No turning back now, he thinks. He uses the pole to test the depth of water to his left. It is much deeper than he is expecting, and he is suddenly lurching forward as the pole becomes half submerged. He tries to counteract the lurch by throwing the weight of his body in the opposite direction. Mick and James cannot believe they are watching a virtual repeat of yesterday's balletic routine. However, this time Andy doesn't fall but somehow ends up on one knee in the middle of the water, with his stick pointing upwards in his left hand.

"Steady on, Andy," says Mick. "It's an entertaining pose, but keeping to your feet would be better."

"You okay, Andy?" enquires James. "Need any help to get upright again?"

Andy rights himself and negotiates his way across the rest of the obstacle without mishap. The right knee of his walking shorts is dripping, and his shin is wet and muddy. Other than that, no damage done. It mightily relieves him to be past the water course.

"Still not got the hang of my stick," he says ruefully.

"You need to use it as an extra leg, not a depth gauge," says James.

"The main thing is you are okay," says Mick, "because for a moment there I thought you were going headlong into the water."

Andy takes off his rucksack to find some wipes to clean his leg and has a long swig of water while he is at it. The leg of his trousers will probably be dry in an hour. He is so glad he is with Mick and James, knowing full well neither will mention the incident to anyone else, so it won't get back to Melissa. He is having second thoughts about the usefulness of using a walking pole and attaches it to the rucksack rather than continue to use it for the rest of the day's walk.

**

The three set off again up the metalled road, which brings them out at a farm; the continuance of the path is unclear. Eventually, they work out going through a gate to the right and dropping below the farm allows them to regain a clearer path. Another splendid section now unfolds as they follow a well-worn grassy path, with a stone wall running parallel to their right. After a further half a mile, they also have the river Rawthey for company again, and beyond, the A683 runs along the valley bottom. The terrain opens before them as they arrive at a huge oxbow manoeuvre of the river. A fast-flowing watercourse from the left also joins at this point. This stretches up the valley, and they can see the white foaming cascade of Cautley Spout spewing water down the hillside to join it.

A footbridge takes them over the watercourse and their path now rises steeply and sharply left over the shoulder of a hill, leaving the Rawthey and A683 behind. Eventually the path levels out and they are now walking along another level grassy track with a tumbledown stone wall stutteringly appearing and then disappearing to their right. A set of ruined cottages provides a suitable spot to stop for lunch. A section of wall has a window space within it, which perfectly frames a wonderful view of the hillside across the other side of the valley.

Whilst they are enjoying their much-needed break and some sustenance, a figure approaches from ahead. He is a man in his eighties, sporting what in its day would have been a rather elegant tweed jacket and a matching flat cap. Underneath the jacket is a white shirt with a cravat at the neck, and he is wearing breeches and knee socks and a pair of heavy looking hiking boots. He stops to exchange greetings and seems keen to engage in conversation. He is walking as far as Cautley Beck before catching the bus back home along the main road.

He asks, "Are you familiar with these parts?" before telling them, "Legend has it the ramshackle buildings where you are dining were once home to royalty. A cousin of Queen Victoria had a tryst with a local girl and commissioned the building of the cottages in order that the pair could meet in secret," he says. "The affair lasted over ten years and when it ended, he allowed her to remain resident here. She lived here until her death in 1915. After that, the cottages were left to fall into disrepair and time and the elements has continued their decline."

It is an interesting tale and after the storyteller has said his goodbyes and gone on his way, the three debate whether or not there is a grain of truth in it.

"He tells a convincing tale," says Andy.

"I don't believe a word of it," says James.

CHAPTER EIGHT

Setting off again becomes a priority, as the sun has gone behind clouds and the sky is much greyer. It is certainly cooler and sitting is no longer the pleasant experience it was at the start of their lunch break. The other priority engendered by James is a realisation that they have now used up all their 'stopping' allowance, and he is getting concerned about them making the scheduled train on time. Unlike Windermere, however, there will be later trains that will get them back to Shipley and Guiseley respectively, but not in time for tea. He knows Sally will make a meal to share and expects Louise will do the same. Whether Melissa will cook tea, he certainly doesn't want Andy arriving home much later than expected given the fragility of his newly found equilibrium.

After a further twenty minutes walking, the hamlet of Artlegarth is reached, just after which there is a fork in the path and a decision needs to be made about which path to take. The left-hand one is signposted 'Public Bridleway to Narthwaite'. They take the right-hand one, which turns out to be the correct decision as they drop and pass Green Barn cottages and finally arrive at Town Head Lane. This now takes them down into Ravenstonedale, where James has stayed and walked from before, with some friends he met whilst undertaking the Pennine Way. They make good progress as they descend into the village and pass the

Westview B&B, where James stayed. At the bottom of the village is the Black Swan Inn and Mick persuades them all to go inside to get a hot drink and to use the facilities.

James knows the route from here and believes it should take an hour and three quarters to get to Kirkby Stephen, so, if they are away by 2.15pm, they should make good time for the train. The hot drinks are welcome as the feel of the day has changed now. All have added extra layers on the last leg of the walk.

They leave the comfort and warmth of the Black Swan and head out of the village and across the A685, before picking up a track that takes them up into Smardale. There are more limestone rocks in evidence as they head up the valley and across open moorland. Ahead, they see the remains of what James believes are several prehistoric villages. These features of the landscape revealing that man, as well as nature, has had a hand in creating its shape.

At a large stile in a stone wall, they bear right and climb the shoulder of Smardale Fell. Several paths seem to meander upwards; motorbikes have churned up one or two, by using them as scrambling rites of passage. There is a summit cairn way over to their right, but James warns against deviating to visit it.

"Just let's keep to the main path," he says.

He is still not completely comfortable with how much time they have left to get to the station. He also knows the others always rely on him to get them to the appointed place on time, irrespective of curved balls thrown at them during the day's walk.

Andy is feeling sad the end of this leg of their

current walking expedition is nearing an end. He thoroughly enjoys the freedom, company and empathy he gets from these two guys, who he may not see much of again until their next walk together. Work rarely facilitates their paths crossing.

As they reach the crest of the shoulder of the hill they have been climbing, they can see Kirkby Stephen in the distance, about two miles away. There are also splendid long-distance views of Wild Boar Fell and Mallerstang Edge to contemplate too. Over to their left, they have a view of Smardale Ghyll and the viaduct that carried the now disused railway from Kirkby Stephen to Sedbergh. The route bears right now and seems to take them away from their intended goal, before it swings left again, and they go through a gate into a field. This drops before rising to meet a second gate, which provides access to a pathway under the railway track.

Now they have undulating fields to cross before a high stile takes them into a wooded area. It is by this time 3.50pm and James is getting panicky. He knows they will be in the village by 4pm, but the station is about three quarters of a mile beyond that along the road to Hawes.

As they exit the wood and can see the town ahead, he suggests 'a little jog' to warm them up before they hit the road. It is exactly 4pm when they reach the road above the village. It is uphill from here to the station and there is no footpath. Even though it is an A-road, the width of it provides just enough room for two cars to pass safely without the need to slow down. Add a pedestrian to the mix and it becomes problematic. Add three pedestrians with rucksacks trying to run as fast as they can after a long day's walk, and it becomes a challenge. Several times, they must leap onto the grass verge to avoid oncoming traffic.

Trying to run in the thick grass and undergrowth of the verge is impossible, so at every opportunity they return to the road in order to make progress. As they arrive at the point where the railway crosses the road, there is an even steeper 100 metre stretch before they reach the station buildings. As they are running up this slope, their train slowly pulls into the station. Dashing onto the platform, they activate the nearest carriage door before the guard blows his whistle and the three collapse in a heap on the floor inside the opening. The doors close behind them and the train pulls away.

"That was bloody close," wheezes Mick.

It takes James and Andy a little longer to get their breath back sufficiently to speak at all. They gather themselves and move down inside the carriage to find somewhere to sit.

"Well, we made it," says James.

"We could have done without a story-telling octogenarian," says Mick.

"And a pirouetting water feature," says Andy.

"And a hot drink in the Black Swan," adds James.

"It's been a brilliant two days as usual," says Andy. "I wouldn't have missed it for the world."

"The next leg means I get to take you two to the Tan Hill Inn."

This is an ambition James has held for a little while, for he believes all serious hikers should stay there at least once during their walking careers. It might not be the plushest pub in the land, but it's the highest and, as he knows first-hand, can be a unique experience.

"Can't wait," says Andy, as the train pulls into Dent station.

* * *

Mick summarises in his head the aspects of the two days walking that he can and will share with Louise. Despite Andy's tumble on Friday and near fall today, there isn't much he needs to avoid. And there's the barbed wire episode and having to run for the train. Despite these minor incidents, Mick realises he has thoroughly enjoyed both the walking and the company of his two friends. Like Andy, he is already looking forward to the next section of their journey.

James is just feeling relieved they caught the train and that the two days passed off with nothing as dramatic as a broken wrist. As they arrive at Ribblehead, it reminds him of another occasion when they had to run for a train.

"Maybe running for the train needs to be a common feature of our outings," he says.

"Er, no," says Mick.

As the train is pulling away from the station, a familiar 'ping' sounds. This time it is James who has a message. It is from Sally informing him she will meet him at Shipley station and give him and Mick a lift home. Louise is aware of the arrangement. She just needs to know what time they are scheduled to arrive. Andy is going to Leeds and will catch the Otley bus from there. Melissa is aware of this arrangement, too.

The message reminds them all to provide details of expected arrival times and for Andy to confirm to Melissa he is all in one piece. It also reminds him of Sally's kind offer to mend the tear in his, or rather Melissa's, cagoule.

"Are you sure she'd be up for it?" he asks.

"Absolutely positive," says James, "and anyway, it will give us an excuse to meet up in a week or two to plan for the next leg. As she rarely wears it, she's hardly likely to miss it, is she?"

"That's true," says a rueful Andy. "What's the next leg again?"

"Kirby Stephen to Reeth," says James, "via the Tan Hill Inn."

"Looking forward to it already!" says Andy.

"There aren't any fallen trees or flooded water courses to negotiate, are there?" asks Mick

CHAPTER NINE

It is a grey and drizzly morning as they leave the train at Kirkby Stephen and head down into the town itself.

"You wouldn't think it's the middle of June," says Andy.

He is wearing the invisibly mended cagoule. Mick has his shorts on with his sunglasses firmly in place, in their familiar spot perched on his head. The only concession to the weather is he is wearing socks under his sandals, rather than his preferred bare foot look.

Andy and James are appropriately togged up for the weather forecast, which, if to be believed, will see low cloud, mist and light rain dominate today. Tomorrow it will improve, with even the promise of afternoon sunshine.

Apart from around 500 metres on paths, the walk into Kirkby Stephen sees them walking single file along the main road. It is 10.30am though, so after the main rush-hour, yet there are still occasions when they must step onto the dew-sodden verge to avoid vehicles coming in both directions, passing them at the same time. Whilst it only takes twenty minutes to get into the town. Mick, in particular, is already on the lookout for a cafe to get a warm drink before the day's proper walking starts.

They find a suitable place to stop, past the sign for the official Coast to Coast route, which will be the starting point for picking up theirs. There is tea for

James and coffees for Andy and Mick, plus some rather splendid looking scones, which are thoroughly enjoyed.

"Can't start a walk on an empty stomach," says Mick.

Emerging into the grey washed skies, James is struck by how much they chime with the grey stone that is a constant feature of every house and building in the town. As they turn to follow the C2C route out of town, they can see mist-shrouded hills ahead. First it's Frank's bridge, then over a brook, skirting between two houses and across a further wooden bridge before emerging onto a path. They see an area of greenery— clearly used by the local dog-walking fraternity— before joining a road.

Tarmac will be their companion for the first mile or so, as they follow the road into and then out of Hartley before their route rises to meet the fells that lie ahead.

"Some marvellous houses around here," says Andy.

"Make the most of them," says James, "because they'll be the last you'll see for the rest of the day."

As they climb up towards Nine Standard Riggs, the swirling mist and persistent drizzle are now joined by strengthening winds. Leaving tarmac behind, they are now following rough, stony tracks before their path becomes slippy grassier steps. Maintaining forward momentum, whilst keeping upright, is becoming more challenging by the moment.

"Exhilarating, isn't it?" says James, as all three stop to have a drink after a steep section.

"I can't believe how bloody cold it is," says Andy, who now has gloves and woolly hat in place, adding,

"Aren't your legs cold, Mick?"

"A little," he begrudgingly admits. "Best to keep going, anyway."

He finishes his drink and gestures to Andy to stow the bottle back into the side pocket of his rucksack. James performs similar manoeuvres for Mick, and Mick for James. As they near the top, the wind is now around gale force nine and standing upright is nigh impossible.

Nine Standard Riggs is so named because it originally boasted nine summit cairns, dotted around the summit plateau. In more recent years, enterprising hikers have used available stones to create one or two more. The largest of the cairns affords enough shelter for the three of them to huddle down and have some respite from the wind. It isn't perfect, but this is the best lunch stop option they are likely to get, and they thrust hands inside rucksacks to bring forth previously prepared, or shop bought delicacies. As usual, James has supplies to feed them all and offers additional culinary options to tempt both Mick and Andy.

"Legend has it," says James, "because they command such a prominent position over Kirkby Stephen and the Eden valley below, they constructed the originals to give the appearance of an English army camped on the summit to deter any marauding Scots!"

"Yeh, right," says Andy, unconvinced.

* * *

After they have sated appetites and warmed up with coffee from flasks, they leave the relative shelter of the cairn to face the force of the wind and rain once more. James has walked this route before and remembers how difficult finding the path from the summit was then, without swirling mists and driving rain. They did still have buffeting winds, though. He heads off in a direction he believes will bring them to the path, but after about 50 metres, suggests they all backtrack and set off again on a different bearing. This time to the right path and, to James's delight, he finds someone has laid one or two flags in places where wet feet were the order of the day in the past.

"Somewhere between the summit and here you passed over into God's own country," says James.

"We're in Yorkshire then," says a pragmatic Mick, who, like James, was born and bred in Lancashire.

Both consider themselves still to be offcumdens, despite having lived in Yorkshire for over thirty years.

They are also now having to negotiate areas of peat bog, and the path meanders to avoid the worst of the cloying stuff. Though, it is impossible to avoid walking on peat or on unstable grassy mounds that rise between it. With the wind still threatening to make them airborne, it takes great concentration and focus to keep going and renders any thoughts of conversation redundant. They almost stumble upon the peaty plateau, where three signposts provide options for their continued progress. Each one has C2C on it. What sets them apart is each suggests the way forward depending on the months of the year they are to be walked along. Although it is only the 23rd of June, James indicates the July/Aug route.

"This takes you in the most direct way to

Whitsundale," he says, which is where they need to get to before deviating from the official C2C again to climb up to the Tan Hill.

The next section is much as James remembers it to be, following a non-existent path between wooden posts placed far enough apart to be visible in pleasant weather. However, in the presence of amoebic floating mists, they are mostly unseen. This means they must strike out in a general direction, before they see the next post, when they can adjust their bearings if they are slightly out. The only words uttered between them on this stretch are when one of them spots a post and brings its existence to the attention of the others.

It's a kind of 'I spy with my little eye' game until their route eventually drops to a beck. James is sure the beck flows through the lines of hills ahead and all along Whitsundale.

"I suggest we stick close to side of the beck for the next stretch and follow the invisible path beside it, rather than following the invisible path between protruding posts."

"Sounds good to me," says Andy.

"Well, if you really know where you are going," adds an uncertain Mick.

Another obstacle now presents itself as large and plentiful clumps of thistle spring up along the banks of the beck. To counteract this, they have playful dippers to watch doing press-ups on rocks amidst the gurgling waters. Overhead, curlews, lapwings and shrike (often heard but seldom seen) entertain them. They take a break at a sheepfold for a snack and some water. James remembers on his last visit here the bodies of several sheep lay against the stone walls of the shelter, where there was a bield from the prevailing winds. However, it was the deep snowdrifts and freezing cold that had been their downfall. He decides against sharing the grisly memory with the others. Mick also uses the stop as an opportunity to change his socks and finally change into his boots. He carefully straps the unwanted sandals to his rucksack and the sodden socks are consigned to an outside pocket.

"You'd better walk in front then," says Andy, adding, "just in case one of your sandals comes loose."

The walk along the side of the beck turns out to be a wise decision. They are out of the worst of the wind. They have clearer visibility in the valley bottom and despite the thistles and the lack of a path, make good progress until they arrive at another signpost that offers the traditional C2C walker, a further three-way choice of routes. James strides confidently on following the signs to Ravens Crag, which they will climb shortly. First, they drop to a farm and campsite, at Raven Seat. Along with a huddle of outbuildings and a couple of cottages, this is Whitsundale's largest settlement.

"I thought you said we wouldn't see any more houses after Hartley?" says Andy.

"Apologies, I forgot about Raven Seat," responds James.

"Well, I for one am very glad to make its acquaintance," says Mick, who has not really enjoyed their journey through little-known wastelands, across peat bogs and down into, and along, desolate Whitsundale.

The farm boasts a sign which heralds 'Cream Teas'

and on the campsite, there is a solitary camper van and beyond it, a guy trying valiantly to erect a tent in the storm. On the other side of the track is a caravan, with a stove throwing out smoke caught and held by the wind in a gyrating quick step. As they pass by its open door, a man pours intensely over the open stove, almost as if he is trying to control which smoke-driven dances play out in the sky.

The official C2C route now follows Whitsundale Beck on its journey south-eastwards towards Keld.

"We need to cross the little road bridge and head up and over Ravens Crag," says James, adding, "so we should be at the Tan Hill Inn in about two hours."

CHAPTER TEN

They turn right at the last building and head up a steep bank, then zig-zag up and over Robert's Seat along a very grassy, spongy, wet and winding faint trail that will eventually see them emerge on to tarmac before they reach the inn itself. From Robert's Seat onwards they have the wind for company as well, albeit not now blowing quiet as strong as it did when they were on Nine Standards Rigg. The rain has stopped, but the sky is parading a pallet of many shades of grey.

"So, what's so special about the Tan Hill Inn?" asks Andy

"Well, apart from being the highest tavern in England and being located roughly where Cumbria, Durham and Yorkshire converge, it is about half-way along the Pennine Way," says James. "It was the first accommodation I booked when I was planning my Pennine Way journey. The accommodation is rough and ready, but the food has been good on both the previous occasions I have stayed there, and they usually have one or two cask ales to sample. If it's a wintry day like today, there'll be a roaring fire going to keep us warm."

"Okay," says Andy, "you market it well!"

"Don't forget Ted Moult," says Mick. He has heard James's tales of the Tan Hill many times before.

"Oh yes, and they used it in that famous advert on TV to advertise Everest Double Glazing," says James.

"The one where a feather drops by the window to prove there are no drafts."

"Ted Moult," says Andy, "there's a blast from the past."

James is still leading the trio, as previously instructed, so either Mick or Andy can deal with any unsolicited sandal separation eventualities. They pass the high point of Raven's Crag and their route turns due east as they drop gently down towards the valley below. After about half a mile, the path returns to a more northerly direction.

"Probably about a mile to go," says James. "Today's walk should only be around twelve miles, but with meanderings through peat bogs, along valley bottoms and a false start from Nine Standards, it may well be nearer thirteen by the time we get there."

There is a ribbon of a road to their right. It clings to and winds its way up the hillside across the valley. The path dips down to meet a watercourse that crosses it ahead. The width of the crossing is too far to leap, but a large boulder sits in the middle of the stream. Its presence has created a larger pool of water to its left, whilst the land drops away more steeply to the right, with water flowing either side of the boulder. This has the effect of creating two separate cascades which merge, in mid-air, about three metres beyond the boulder before continuing as one down the hillside.

"Interesting little feature," says Mick.

He takes a confident stride onto the boulder with one foot, his momentum taking him across the obstacle, so he lands safely on the other foot, on the opposite bank. James is next and having observed the way his friend negotiated the crossing, he too confidently strides onto the large stone with his right foot, but the stone moves under him and instead of the momentum taking him to the other side, it throws him to the left. He struggles in mid-air to regain some balance, but somehow ends up on his back in the pool of water to the left of the boulder, like an upturned turtle, and utters forth a string of obscenities. Mick ahead misses the spectacle, but Andy gets to witness it in crazy detail.

"Nice one, James," he says.

"Did you see it?" asks a spluttering and now semi-upright James. "It bloody moved."

"Not half as dramatically as you did," suggests Andy. He is enjoying the fact it is James and not him who has suffered a fall from grace.

The rucksack prevents any major physical harm from the fall and luckily the rain cover is still in place, although it hasn't been raining for the past two hours.

"At least the internal contents, including my change of clothing for this evening, won't be wet," says James. He is regaining his composure and checking the rucksack to be sure of his statement.

Mick turns at the noise of the commotion and the three use the unscheduled delay to have a last drink of water before heading onwards. Andy delights in describing James's dramatic and acrobatic 'dying swan' routine to Mick, completely exaggerating every aspect.

"There's the Tan Hill," says James, pointing to the top half and roof of a building protruding over a rise ahead.

Their route, however, drops first and the 'vision' of

their night's resting place is lost. A final pull, crossing a rickety bridge; two planks of wood, across a stream, leads to them finally reach tarmac, before they become re-acquainted with a fuller vista of the Tan Hill Inn.

* * *

Within the sanctuary of the place, it is as James remembers from before, perhaps a bit more rough and ready. The motley crew of staff, who serve like shipmates on this vessel of the higher fells, seem mainly to come from Poland or Albania. There's even a Greek. The hostess confirms their booking and shows them rooms and places where damp clothes and boots can be 'air-dried'.

Despite his beached turtle routine, James is feeling very pleased with himself for having finally dragged his two walking comrades to the Tan Hill, particularly after a warm shower, a change of clothing, and a place is found for his boots in the drying room.

This also serves as the linen room, laundry room and an overflow store for the Tan Hill and is a narrow alleyway that runs on the other side of the corridor to their rooms. They gain entry to it by the entrance to the bunk room, where up to sixteen people can sleep. This also serves as a washroom area for the bunkroom, with the entrance to the 'drying room' being immediately behind a small door to the right. This means you can open the door on someone in the throes of having a wash and have to apologise and return later, something Andy experiences on his first visit.

He is feeling relieved at having survived the day

with no mishaps and is looking forward to an evening spent in pleasant company, in front of the roaring fire and with a plate of the good food promised him by James.

Andy knows his anxieties about his relationship with Melissa will be enquired about this evening. Things have taken a step backwards since the previous leg of the walk and he doesn't know how to deal with his feelings of impending doom. He has convinced himself Melissa wants to leave. They have talked a lot about moving to another house ostensibly to save money, and about what changes each may make to their lifestyles once the children have left home. Such conversations are rational exchanges. At other times, they end with him believing Melissa has an ulterior motive. If he keeps quiet, he gets down. If he voices his concerns, she gets frustrated with him. Being away from Melissa for a couple of days, with two good friends who he can offload to, is a real pressure release valve for him and he recognises this is as important to him as the enjoyment he gets from the walking itself.

After his initial attempt at trying to utilise the drying room, it is second time lucky, and he can eventually join James and Mick in the bar room. It is Mick who asks about Melissa first and he apologetically updates them both about how things are. Mick believes Louise has mellowed a little in relation to what she refers to as his 'walking adventures'. Sally has long since accepted James's penchant for going off walking. She has her own interests too, but does insist they spend some quality time together as well.

There are three people in the bar, with a member of

staff putting in an occasional appearance to make sure everyone is okay and to serve anyone needing a glass replenishing. They have been sitting and sharing thoughts from home for about fifteen minutes when the door opens and a couple in their late fifties come through. They commence a dialogue with the member of staff about their booking for this evening. They have walked twenty-two miles in the rain, along the Pennine Way, and are very much in need of a rest and some warmth, a feeling James knows only too well. The register is checked, and they are told there is no confirmed booking in their name and there is no room in the inn tonight, unless they are prepared to share with fourteen others in the bunk room.

Clearly, this is not an option they wish to consider, but neither is carrying on, with the next stopping over point along the Pennine Way being some eight miles further on. Their belligerence results in a second member of staff emerging onto the scene, and the debates and arguments flow back and forth. Eventually it transpires he had booked the room, but in her name. This little drama occupies others in the room for around ten minutes before it is satisfactorily resolved, and the couple are shown to their room in order to change out of their wet and muddy walking gear.

"It doesn't seem to be fully booked," says Andy. "Exactly how many people can it accommodate?"

"I think there are six twin rooms. We've got two of them. Then there's the bunk room and there is also a bunk barn separate to the main building," James says.

"Well," says Mick, "even if the three people in the bar are all staying tonight in separate rooms and the couple who've just arrived are in one, we've only seen two other people in the building, so there must be plenty of room."

At that moment the door opens and for the next five minutes, a group of around a dozen somewhat unfit cyclists stagger bowlegged into the room. It turns out they have cycled from Newcastle and will return tomorrow via Reeth, Richmond and Darlington. Theirs is an annual pilgrimage, started several years ago, that most of the party seem honour bound to continue. Suddenly, what was a quiet and sleepy room is teeming with sweaty men in lycra, mud splattered legs and Geordie accents. Some need to sit down or hold a piece of furniture to stay upright. Three of them are busy using inhalers to steady their breathing.

After they have vacated the space to make their way up to the bunk room, relative calm returns to the bar.

"They'll be a bloody long time if they've all got to use the single multi-purpose wash-room," says Andy.

A fire is laid ready in the grate, but there is no sign of anyone taking a match to it. Mick goes to the bar to order some more drinks and politely requests the fire be lit. A rather burly tattooed woman emerges from the back room and throws coal onto the unlit fire directly from a large scuttle. She then reappears with a Calor gas canister, which she connects to a huge flame thrower, with which she seeks to light the fire. She plays the jet of flame over the coals for a good while before seeming satisfied. The coals may glow, but there is no sign of a flame and before long, the glowing subsides, and the fire remains unlit.

She re-emerges and repeats the procedure this time

for a little longer, ultimately with the same result. Finally, she returns and douses the coals in some substance squirted from a bottle and then puts the flame-thrower to work again. An enormous ball of flame rises from the coals before it reduces to a flicker. She has at least ignited some of the paper and wood beneath the dump of coals. Some of them are keeping their red glow, whilst others have turned ashen pale.

"I think we may have a fire at last," says Andy.

"If the food is as good as the entertainment, we'll be laughing," says Mick.

"We've had the Lithuanian flame thrower, it'll be the Polish juggler next, followed by the Greek plate smashing," suggests James, adding, "The first time I was here everybody went out to watch a sheep being sheared in the porch."

"Now I know why you really wanted us to stay here," says Andy.

A little calm is restored, and the cyclists filter back down to the bar and the Pennine Way walkers return too and stand with their backs to the still fledgling inferno.

"Time to order some food," says Mick. "All this flame throwing has made me peckish."

"Nothing to do with having walked thirteen miles then?" says James.

"I thought you said it was twelve," says Andy.

* * *

When the food arrives, it is very basic and nowhere near as good as James remembered it to have been. It is at least edible and fills a hole and leads to an interesting post eating conversation about the best accommodation and food they have experienced at the end of a day's walk. They unanimously agree after considering several options The Eagle and Child at the end of the penultimate leg of the Dales Way and again after completing the Kentmere round takes the first prize. Even accepting they waited twenty minutes before realising they had to order food from the bar the first time they stayed there.

They are now drinking malts and, in Andy's case, a gin and having to strip down to tee-shirts as the heat of the fire, and fourteen Geordie cyclists, transform the room into a warm cocoon. The Pennine Way walkers went to bed an hour ago and two of the three people who were at the bar when they arrived have also retired. The effects of the heat and possibly the day's walking finally takes its toll and they decide to leave the cyclists and the remaining original resident, who is half-propped, half-slumped against the bar. It has been a very enjoyable day.

As they rise to leave their seats, a 'ping' is heard, and Andy tries hard not to look at his phone but is compelled to succumb.

"She'll have had a hard day with the kids," he says. "She wouldn't be texting if it wasn't something really serious or she's been brooding on stuff."

Sure enough, as soon as Andy scans the message, he can tell there is no immediate crisis and the words he is reading are an outpouring of Melissa's frustration, cultivated by an evening of stewing on things Andy said before his 'time away'.

"Ah well," he says, "at least I've got another full day with you guys tomorrow. Sleep well."

He retires to his room, whilst Mick and James go to theirs.

"It takes the edge off things, doesn't it?" says James.

"It does for Andy," says Mick. "He beats himself up so."

The two continue to discuss their friend and his situation for a further half hour before tiredness sets in and lights are switched off.

CHAPTER ELEVEN

It takes several visits to the washroom to gain access to the drying room before the three have retrieved all their stuff. The Geordie bikers keep having to be apologised to as their morning ablutions get interrupted. It isn't just guests trying to get in there either, as staff members need to fetch clean linen and towels. One staff member has even set up an ironing board at one end of the drying area to reduce the number of creases in some sheets, which have been tumble dried.

Breakfast is in a room at the opposite end of the bar to the open fire, which is still smouldering and giving off heat at 8am when they get downstairs. The room is full of an assortment of different tables—round, square and some larger rectangular ones. They have been arranged throughout the room with little regard for creating sensible walkways between them. Most of the dining chairs are of odd shapes, with many too bulky for the space. As all staff have to pass in and between such arrangements, both to take orders and subsequently deliver breakfast requirements, many diners have to frequently adjust their position to facilitate the safe delivery of plates, hot tea or coffee pots to the relevant tables.

Most of the bikers are already seated by the time James, Andy and Mick enter the room and find a table that requires one of them to sit in the unused and open fireplace at the far side. It is Mick who draws the short straw. Having just got themselves suitably arranged, it is pointed out, cereals and fruit juices are self-service and are on a table in the opposite corner. Mick extricates himself from the table in time to meet a server coming the other way with two English breakfasts for two of the bikers, who are sitting furthest from the kitchen. They each effectively undertake a three-point turn to facilitate safe passage. Having selected some cereal and a juice, Mick waits until the coast is clear before edging his way back. Both James and Andy now repeat the manoeuvre, the latter's return being immediately preceded by the delivery of tea and coffee to their table. Ten minutes has already elapsed since they first sat down.

"It's a good job we're not in a hurry this morning," says Andy.

By the time their cooked breakfasts arrive, most of the bikers have left and chairs can be pushed to tables to create a little more wriggle room. The two Pennine Way walkers are just finishing their breakfast too, but not before James has engaged them in conversation about his own experience and discussed with them their journey to date and plans for the next few days. They are heading as far as Middleton-in-Teesdale today, which is where he stayed after the Tan Hill. He wishes them good luck, and shakes hands with them both before they leave the dining room.

Apart from the last two biker stragglers, they now have the dining room to themselves. There is no sign of the man who was propping up the bar when they retired last night, and they don't see him prior to their departure, either.

"How are things back home?," Mick asks Andy.

"We have had civil contact this morning," he responds.

"How long did it take you to retrieve your boots and any other stuff you had in the drying room this morning?" Andy asks, clearly wanting to change the subject.

"About three trips and fifteen minutes," says James.

"Did you meet Irena?" says Andy.

"Who is Irena?" says Mick.

"Oh, she's a very helpful Polish member of staff, who was ironing sheets in the drying room. She helped me gather all my stuff together and carried some of it to my room, so I didn't have to make two trips."

"Sounds like you're on a winner there," says James.

"Actually, she's probably in her late sixties, short and a little dumpy, but preferable to the tattooed flame thrower," says Andy, "and certainly the most helpful staff member I've met."

Eventually, the three of them are the last to leave the dining room and go up to their rooms to finish packing, encountering the shortly to depart motley crew of Geordie cyclists as they all retrieve their means of transport from a shed behind the inn as they prepare to set off on their long journey home.

"Good luck," says James.

"Aye, some of us'll need it," is the response from one of the fitter specimens.

* * *

It is about 9.30am by the time the three of them are ready to leave. The wind has blown away the mists and grey skies of yesterday, but it is still chilly, and the sun is struggling to break through the clouds.

"How far today, James?" asks Mick.

"It should be twelve miles," says James, "route finding on the first stretch is the major challenge."

What James should have said is there simply isn't a route to find for the first mile and a half. It starts off well enough, as they head east along the road signposted to Reeth, go over a cattle grid and then shortly afterwards follow a path to the right, which soon disappears altogether. James points way ahead to a hill that rises from west to east.

"There's a path along that ridge which we need to get to," he says. "According to the map, there is a track that should take us from the Tan Hill to join it. However, there were five of us last time I did this, and we had four compasses and 2 GPS devices between us, and we never found it. So, my suggestion is we don't even bother trying to look for it and just head straight for the ridge. There will be times when we will have to deviate, as there are swampy areas and peat bogs to negotiate, as well as some unseen hollows."

"You sell it almost as well as you sold us the Tan Hill," says Andy.

"Yes, and that didn't quite hit the mark," says Mick.

"The food and the accommodation might not have been as good as last time I was there, but you've got to admit the entertainment was novel," said James.

It takes well over an hour before they reach the

relative sanctuary of the slopes of the hill that have been their target for so long. Both Mick and James have been up to their knees in a slimy peat bog. Andy has wet feet from being submerged to below the knee in what he thought was a shallow puddle, which turned out to be more of a submerged lake. They have tried surfing grassy tussocks, to avoid the morasses that lay between them, clambered up and down sudden dips and steep rises, gone left, gone right, tried zigzags, and eventually resigned themselves to walking in a straight line, whatever it threw at them.

They slump on the first firm earth they have experienced for what seems like a lifetime to recover and attempt to clean away most of the evidence of their 'crossing'.

"Wet wipe or three," says Mick, seeking to wipe away the smears of oozing dark mud that coat both his legs.

James uses some of the water from his bottle and the socks he wore yesterday to clean away the worst of the mud and finishes his cleansing activities with the aid of his micro towel and his trusty Swiss army knife. The latter is used to scrape away mud from his boots. Mick has changed out of his and is now wearing his favoured sandals.

"I trust there is no more terrain of that ilk?" he asks.

"No, we're past the worst of it," says James.

"Does that mean we've still the best of it to come?" says Mick. "Thank goodness Louise isn't with us. She'd be wanting you 'sectioned' for taking us on a route through such a wilderness."

"Aye, and you and I, too, for following him," says Andy.

The path along the ridge is indistinct, but after what they have just endured, it feels as clear as a three-lane motorway. There are even occasional little cairns to reassure them they are walking along a recognised footpath. It is a cold and blustery wind, but at least the mist and rain have disappeared and, so long as they keep moving, the unseasonable chill in the air is not unpleasant. The lack of mist means they now have extensive views of both the south and the east, the latter being their direction of travel for the next three or four miles.

"What's that ridge of a hill in the far distance?" asks Andy.

"The one to the right is probably Fremington Edge," says James. "We undulate a bit before dropping into Arkengarthdale and then we'll have the 'edge' to our left as we meander down to Reeth."

"Arkengarthdale," said Mick. "I've stayed with Louise in a cottage there. It's a splendid little valley, although not as well frequented as some of the other dales. One or two friendly pubs, if I remember correctly."

"Quite right, Mick," said James. "We found a couple of nice one's last time I walked this route."

"Something to compensate us for the first hour and a half's walk then," said Andy.

James has stopped by now to consult the map more intently, in order to more fully respond to Andy's question.

"So," he says, "that's Arkengarthdale Moor in the

mid-distance, with Cleasby Hill behind it. We're currently on Great Scollit Hill and are now heading towards the highest point of the day on West Moor. After that, it's pretty much downhill all the way to Reeth."

As they drop and negotiate their way round and through the grouse moors, before the gentle ascent of West Moor, the sun comes out and for the rest of the day is almost a constant companion. It doesn't generate enough heat, however, for any of them to want to shed a layer. Even the hardy Mick has his cagoule in place, albeit over his shorts and sandals. Coming down the other side of the gentle slopes of West Moor, their path seems to disappear again in an area of peat, heather and scrubland. James points out a clear path about half a mile ahead and to their right and suggests they head in that general direction.

"No point wasting time and energy trying to find a pretty indistinct path, when we can clearly see where we need to be ahead," he says.

That theory is soon made redundant though as their route drops and they are once more having to negotiate grassy tussocks between peaty hollows, or wade through tangling heathers, which rise above their knees. All of this means each must focus entirely on where the next footfall is to be made and for the next ten minutes, each is lost in the simple task of maintaining forward momentum until they can make clearer ground. Mick is taking his time; maintaining an upright posture becomes a challenge as the ground under the tangle of vegetation beneath his feet threatens to throw him off balance.

"Just concentrate, keep calm. Solid ground is not far ahead," are words he repeats over and over to himself.

James stops every ten feet and manoeuvres to scan the horizon, both to pick the route for the next ten 'paces' and to find the elusive path ahead. Finally, as he looks up, he can see the path about one hundred metres away ahead and to the right.

"Clear path ahead, just follow me now," he shouts, turning round as he does so.

There is no sign of either Andy or Mick. For about thirty seconds he feels completely alone in the landscape, before he spots Mick about fifty metres away.

"Work your way towards me, Mick," he says.

"Right-o," says Mick, feeling mightily relieved to be almost free of the tangle of heather roots, and to have James clearly in his sights again.

He joins James, who points out the clear path ahead, a short distance away.

"I don't remember that stretch from last time," says James. "We must have bypassed it somehow."

As they both turn and survey again the area, there is still no sign of Andy.

"Where is he?" asks Mick.

"Good question."

They both shout his name in unison and the wind seems to carry their voices into the air. A startled grouse breaks cover and with a manic flapping of wings and a persistent, grumbling cry heads westwards on an erratic flight path. However, there is no sign or sound of Andy.

A Very Alternative Coast to Coast

***

Soon after Andy starts his negotiation of the peaty, tussock strewn and heather clad area, he stops to answer a call of nature and his phone rings. Melissa. She is in both an apologetic but excited mood. She has been researching undertaking courses of professional training and has decided she really fancies training as an occupational therapist. From her investigations, she believes she meets the entry requirements, and she has already, this morning, sent off for details of courses within the Yorkshire region. Also, Claire, their eldest daughter, has had a 'puppy-love crisis'. Melissa sat down and had a positive mother-daughter conversation with her and she is feeling great about this, too.

If he had been at home, Andy knew Claire would have come to him to 'chew the cud' on the matter and this would have irked Melissa. She and Claire, like many mums and teenaged daughters, didn't have the best of relationships. Melissa had been known to brood, internalise, and 'beat herself up' about such matters.

Melissa is really looking forward to his return this evening. Andy agrees to help and support her with any applications she wants to pursue. As he finishes the phone-call, he wonders whether this is another of Melissa's life-change fantasies, or whether she is truly as serious about her proposed career change as she sounded on the phone.

He suddenly realises he must have been on his mobile for the past ten minutes and he can no longer see either Mick or James. He sets off again, trying to hurry across terrain that does everything it can to prevent smooth passage.

***

James and Mick decide to at least make their way to the start of the clear path before resuming their shouts to locate Andy. Once there, James suggests to Mick if Andy doesn't appear within the next five minutes, Mick should stay put, whilst he goes back to find him.

"He can't be far away, can he? We were all together fifteen minutes ago."

Mick is just about to confirm his agreement when he catches sight of Andy, careering crazily towards them from way over to their left.

"Over here, Andy," he calls. "Are you alright?"

Andy doesn't answer immediately as he uses all his energy to propel himself forward, but then he stops about fifty metres away to respond.

"Phone call from Melissa," he says, "tell you more when I get to you."

CHAPTER TWELVE

When the three are finally back together again, Andy has to re-live the conversation with Melissa and has a snack and some water. Further down the footpath in the far distance there is what looks like a building and James remembers there are some former mine workings ahead they must pass through.

"Only about an hour until we hit tarmac down in Arkengarthdale," he says.

The footpath remains clear now and hugs the contours of the valley as they make their way down Great Punchard Ghyll. They are suddenly aware of the coolness of the biting wind again, as their way is more exposed. Some of the sturdy stone-built structures of the former mining area are in good condition, and there are one or two soil heaps in evidence.

Further down, at a ford across the beck, is a well-constructed little bridge. There is an opportunity to clamber down and onto a steep grassy bank to one-side of the bridge, to gain some respite from the wind. It also provides a good place to stop for a snack and another swig or two of water.

"You can't help but marvel at the ingenuity and determination of the men involved in mining coal in such an inaccessible place," says Andy.

"Incredulity and foolhardiness, don't you mean?" says Mick.

"It would have been hard work for not much reward at any rate," James adds.

"I'd have thought it was lead, not coal, that was mined up here," says Mick.

"It was at first," says James, "but the bottom fell out of the lead market just before the First World War, whereas they carried on mining coal until about the time of the Second World War."

"Is it usual to be mining for both lead and coal in the same place?" asks Andy.

"I think it was during the lead mining time that seams of coal were discovered," says James. "I think there was another third mineral mined for too, but I can't remember which one."

"Unusual for you, not to have such a detail to hand." Mick is smiling.

"True, must be the Alzheimer's setting in. I can tell you though, in the lead mining days, they dug several of what were called 'bell pits' to get to lead seams, and lots of tunnels were dug. Some of them ran for as much as six miles underground."

"Get away!" says Andy.

"Time to move on," says Mick.

After crossing the bridge, the path bears round to the right before dropping more steeply down into Arkengarthdale. They can now see the ribbon of road they will shortly join.

"Where does that road come from and go to?" says Mick.

"It's the road we left shortly after leaving the Tan Hill and it goes down the valley now all the way to Reeth," says James.

Immediately, he has uttered these words he can almost predict what will follow. He inwardly curses his stupidity, knowing he should have said something more like 'I'm not sure. I'll have to consult the map.' He's usually very good at keeping secrets.

"Do you mean to say," says Mick, "we could have just kept to the road, missed all that crap you've dragged us through and probably got to Reeth even sooner than we will?"

"Bloody hell!" says Andy.

"I thought the whole point of these walks of ours was that we have a bit of a challenge to overcome to make them worthwhile," says James, trying hard to regain his composure.

"Known about, anticipated and prepared for challenges are one thing," says Mick, "but deliberately heading across god forsaken peat bogs with no clear paths is entirely something else!"

"Steady on you two," says Andy, drawing on the newfound positivity from his talk with Melissa. "We're here, in one piece, and we will have lots more to reminisce about when we recall today's walk, in future, over a pint.

"Speaking of which," says James, "the first pub we come to is only about half a mile down the road. The drinks are on me."

They all break out into laughter and the 'alternative road route' doesn't get mentioned again for the rest of the day.

* * *

The sun seems warmer, and the valley bottom provides more shelter from the wind, as they reach the road just south of the settlement of Whah, and head down to the sanctuary of the pub promised by James. Just before they reach it, they pass a road junction with a turnoff to the left, signposted to Thwaite and Barnard Castle. The pub is the CB Inn, which is clearly signed as they near it. Almost before Andy or Mick can ask the obvious question, Paul informs them the CB stands for Charles Bathurst, and sure enough as they turn past the first gable end to find the main entrance, a larger sign across the frontage proclaims, 'The Charles Bathurst Inn'.

They take off rucksacks and debate whether to sit outside at one of the picnic tables or go inside.

"I'll get us some drinks and bring some menus out, whilst you two determine whether it's warm enough to sit in the sun," says James. With that, he heads inside.

"I'm really pleased this morning's news from home is so positive," says Mick.

"Yeh, I can't quite believe it, really. I'm pleased she and Claire could share something that would ordinarily have been difficult for them to talk about."

"I'm sure Sally worked as an OT for several years. I'm sure if Melissa continues to want to pursue that as a new career, James will be happy to speak to her and to provide any advice he can."

"What advice is that?" says James, emerging from the pub with three pints on a tray, and some menus tucked under his arm.

"Just saying to Andy, Sally used to work as an OT," says Mick.

"True," says James, adding, "so if she's serious about it, Andy, I'd be happy to discuss things. There's a brilliant course at York which confusingly, if I remember correctly, comes under the auspices of the University at Leeds. I can always find out more and, as well as Sally, there are one or two former OT colleagues she's still in touch with."

Lunch options are chosen, and they sit outside sipping their pints to await its arrival.

"Didn't Charles Bathurst have something to do with Cromwell?" asks Mick. "I have a recollection from when we stayed in a cottage near here that he was a prominent figure from the seventeenth century and seemed to own quite a lot in the local area."

"Spot on Mick," says James. "He was Oliver Cromwell's doctor. He owned lots of property in the area and even owned the lead mining company that mined the area we came past. I believe it carried on as CB and Co 'till it finally shut down before the war."

The sun temporarily finds refuge behind a cloud and before their food arrives, they make the sensible decision to eat inside.

Emerging well fed and in good humour, it pleases them to discover the sun is once more well set and they carry on down the road towards a cluster of buildings on either side of the road. They mark Arkengarthdale C of E School and the three ruminate on how many pupils a school in such a rural location will have and, in turn, how many teachers they will need to meet the educational needs of those students.

As they are passing the school, a group of four cyclists are heading up towards Whaw and Mick, who is also a keen cyclist, as well as a runner, remarks how the lanes round here must make for good cycling.

"I think the Tour de France route comes this way," says James.

"I think the climb past the CB Inn and up to the Tan Hill is called the 'Stang' and is said to be one of the best cycling climbs in Europe," says Mick, remembering another fact from his previous stay in the area.

"Steady on," says an impressed Andy, "you'll be putting James out of his job as 'tour guide' at this rate."

"I can't imagine those 'Geordie cyclists' coming up this way," says Mick.

"No, but I bet they cycled down it from the Tan Hill though," James comments.

"I wonder where they are now," says Andy, still cogitating on Mick's description of the 'Stang'.

"Probably be in Richmond, or nearly in Darlington by now," says Mick.

A little further on and they enter the hamlet of High Green and beyond it the larger settlement of Langthwaite. James suggests they have a drink in the Red Lion, where he had a pleasant interlude on his last walking of today's route.

"After Langthwaite we are off the road and have a pretty walk along the river as it meanders down into Reeth. You'll also be able to see the impressive escarpment ridge of Fremington edge to your left."

This time the warmth of the sun is enough for them to enjoy their pints outside. The Red Lion also serves as the Post Office and corner shop for the village and the local area.

A Very Alternative Coast to Coast

Sitting outside the Red Lion in the sunshine and enjoying the second very drinkable pint of the day provides an excellent opportunity to reflect on this section of the walk. Suddenly, the rain and high winds of yesterday and then following often unseen route markers to find their way into and along Whitsundale, followed by their night at the Tan Hill, seem pleasurable memories. Even this morning's near impossible route-finding challenges to finally drop into Great Punchard Ghyll, before finally emerging onto the road below Whaw, are assuming more 'glowing' attributes.

The hour's walk along Arkle beck as it twists, turns and gurgles its way down the valley is pure joy. They cross fields, negotiate stiles, avoid cattle, share greetings with fellow ramblers and take in the majesty of the towering escarpment of Fremington edge high on their left.

Conversation now turns to 'travel' arrangements for their return journey home from Reeth and to how much time they may have to explore the village.

"We should have at least an hour and a half in Reeth before we must catch the last bus of the day to Richmond at ten past five. If we miss it, there isn't another one until tomorrow."

"Where do we head to from Richmond? Northallerton?" asks Andy.

"No, actually and somewhat counter-intuitively, we catch the bus to Darlington, where we get the train back to Leeds," says James.

"I'm sure it all makes perfect sense, and you will have worked it out to the finest detail," says Andy.

The track follows the rise and fall of the land and hugs the riverbank where it can. At one point, they must head up a quick rise and away from the river to avoid a clump of trees whose roots seem to visibly grip the contours of the land to anchor themselves against all eventualities.

* * *

It is exactly three thirty when they arrive in the picturesque village of Reeth, and first off, locate the bus stop they will need to be at, to catch the 'little white' bus to Richmond. Having explored the shops that bind two sides of the green and square in Reeth, a decision is made to have a sit down, cup of tea and maybe some cake and at four they are all seated in the Overton House Cafe. The cake is extremely moreish, the staff friendly and the hot mugs of tea very satisfying. They make a note to call here again, next time they are in Reeth. A group of four cyclists arrive and, after parking their cycles outside, enter and seem equally pleased with their choices of beverage and cake. In conversation with the accommodating staff and the cyclists and in sharing stories of their adventures and plans, they are oblivious to the time. Suddenly, Mick looks out of the window across the green to where they must catch their bus.

"Isn't that our little white bus?" he says.

A glance at watches shows it is five past five and Mick and James head for the door and out into the sunlight, exchanging fond farewells, whilst Andy settles the bill and then sprints after them. Luckily, the bus driver spots the hurrying forms of James and Mick as they race across the green to the bus stop and kindly awaits their arrival. Recovering, they stagger on board and point out the third member of their party who is now also sprinting across the green towards them.

"Cutting it fine are we?," he says.

It is a moment or two before either of them has breath enough to respond.

"Profuse apologies," says James, "we lost track of time. We actually arrived in Reeth about an hour and a half ago, in plenty of time."

"I saw you bursting forth from the cafe on the far side of the green," he says. "They do a damn good bacon butty there in the mornings, too."

"Thank you for waiting," says Andy, as he too boards the bus, pays his fare and plonks himself down on a seat.

The little bus takes off with a lurch and soon they are hurtling along the country lanes towards Richmond. The driver swerves occasionally to avoid a pot-hole and tells them 'it's great the Tour de France is coming to the area, as all these ruddy holes are going to get filled in, to make it a smooth ride for all them cyclists.'

If the calmness and the tranquillity of the Overton House seemed a perfect place to relax at the end of a day's walk, the twenty-five minute bus ride into Richmond is more like a fairground ride designed to test the theory of gravity and their ability to withstand being shaken around inside a moving object, whilst trying to remain in a seated position. Their gratitude to the driver for waiting for them in Reeth has almost evaporated by the time they emerge all wobbly legged onto the solid pavement in Richmond.

Their connection to Darlington is due in ten minutes, but after their nearly missed bus experience in Reeth, they decide to stay put at the bus stop.

"We'll probably have time to explore Richmond a little, on the next leg of the walk," says James, as if speaking for them all.

"Is this where we'll overnight?" says Andy.

"Sure is."

The bus to Darlington is a 'proper' bus and the ride a much smoother and calmer experience. They have only about ten minutes to wait before the train for Leeds pulls in and they can relax in even more comfortable seating and reflect again on the experience of the last two days.

James explains whilst the next leg of their alternative coast to coast walk will be from Reeth to Northallerton, with an overnight in Richmond, he needs to do more thinking and planning around the last leg, in order to avoid a very long walk on one of the days.

"The plan is to get from Northallerton to Osmotherley, before picking up the Cleveland Way and finishing the walk at Saltburn."

The three have walked the Cleveland Way before and really enjoyed that stretch.

"The problem is working out where we can overnight. There is nowhere around the half-distance mark that has accommodation. I'll continue to research and keep you posted."

"Richmond looked extremely pleasant," says Andy.

"If we can get to Reeth early enough, I wouldn't

mind starting off with a bacon butty and a mug of tea at the Overton House cafe," says Mick.

"Sounds like a plan," says James.

CHAPTER THIRTEEN

The following spring...

The three of them are on the train to Northallerton, having all linked up at Leeds station. They have barely found seats and stowed their rucksacks before Andy turns to James.

"So, what's this big issue you need to run past us before we walk then, James?"

"Well," says James, "you know when we met up last November to discuss today's walk and I explained for the rest of our journey to the east coast, we'd have to do Sundays and Mondays, rather than Fridays and Saturdays?"

"It might have got mentioned," says Mick, "but we all know we met up to share a pint or two, have a bite to eat and have a catch up."

"I know that, but all the same, it's Sunday today, and that's because I asked, and you both agreed, to change our walking days, as Sally and I now have grandparent duties on a Friday."

"What of it?" says Andy. "Changing days wasn't a big issue then, and it isn't now."

He was already growing impatient with James, who texted him a couple of days ago to confirm all the transport and accommodation arrangements for this leg of their walk, but shared there was an issue he needed to discuss on the train before they started walking.

"Well, back in November, I checked all the transport arrangements and, according to my research, getting to Reeth by public transport on a Sunday was not a problem."

"Yes, I remember you saying," says Mick.

"When I was completing all the arrangements a couple of weeks ago, I discovered you can no longer get to Reeth on a Sunday, not till the height of summer, anyway." He left the statement hanging in the air for the gist of it to sink in before continuing. "I have explored the option of a taxi from Northallerton to Reeth, which will more than double the cost of this trip. It's too much to pay, and I think there may be a better plan."

"Have you hired us cycles," asks Andy, "or a horse and cart?"

"I haven't hired anything. I thought it might be a laugh to walk this leg backwards!"

Again, the statement is followed by a pause as James waits for responses to his preposterous, but in his opinion 'bloody genius', plan.

"Walk backwards?" says Mick.

"Walk into the wind." There is a pause. "And rain!"

Andy is watching the raindrops streaming down the window of the carriage they are sitting in and has checked the weather forecast for today and tomorrow and is aware they may experience some rain for an hour or two this morning.

"Look, I know you were both looking forward to a bacon butty in the Overton House cafe, but if we walk from Northallerton to Richmond today, we can be in

Reeth tomorrow in plenty of time to enjoy the culinary delights there, before catching the little white bus back to Richmond."

"You should have discussed this significant change with us before," says Mick.

He isn't sure he is comfortable with the purity of undertaking a linear walk in stages, where one of the stages is walked back to front. Or maybe it's more he isn't sure Louise will approve. He is already thinking about how he will explain the sudden change of plan to her. Maybe he can say he knew about it all along and he thought it was a splendid and extremely quirky idea? Maybe he could even suggest to her it was his idea? A practical solution to what at first may have seemed like an insurmountable problem.

"I would have mentioned it before today, but I thought it would cause another postponement and it's so bloody difficult getting dates sorted when the three of us can synchronise diaries."

"Is Sally aware of the alternative route?" asks Mick.

"No, she'd have insisted I discussed it with you both beforehand, wouldn't she?"

Mick is at least relieved that a chance conversation between her and Sally will not sabotage the opportunity to claim credit for the change of plan with Louise.

"I don't suppose it really matters which way we cover the route, as long as we cover it," says Andy.

It quite relieves him in some ways they will walk sooner rather than later. He wasn't particularly looking forward to the two bus journeys that would have probably followed on from their arrival in Northallerton in order to get to Reeth.

As the train pulls into York station, they can finally put James's 'big issue' behind them for the moment and catch up on each other's family news.

As they leave York the day is fine, but the light greys are turning decidedly darker in places. It will be touch and go whether they have rain by the time they get to Northallerton. Andy is also keen to talk about home life, whilst they are still all together on the train.

"Melissa has got a place on the Occupational Therapy professional training course and starts in September," he proudly states. "Things have been a lot better for some time now and she is really looking forward to the course."

"That's brilliant," says Mick.

"On both scores," echoes James.

"She wore the cagoule a few months ago too and didn't notice the invisibly stitched pocket repair. Sally really did a brilliant job there, James."

"Yeah, she's a diamond in lots of ways."

"The next couple of days should be a lot less taxing than any of the previous legs of this challenge. Just need the weather to be kind, too."

As if to prove the point, James fishes out a map and lays it out on the table to provide a quick overview of the route they will take. As a voice from the ether announces the next station stop will be Northallerton, the map is quickly folded away and the three gather belongings together, retrieve rucksacks from the overhead luggage shelves and rise in unison to gather in the door well, as the train slows and finally stops at the station.

* * *

It is spitting with rain in Northallerton as they wind their way out of the station and get their bearings. James pulls out his favourite flat cap, a suede waterproof one he bought at the Harrogate Flower Show last year, rather than put the hood of his cagoule up.

"Nice cap," says Andy.

"Yes, cost me a bit, but it's the best flat cap I've ever owned!"

As they turn the corner, the drizzle thickens to heavy rain and they all shiver and hunker down into their waterproofs.

"I hope it will not be another 'Filey' day," says Mick.

It's too wet to get a map out, but luckily James remembers one of the first places they will pass through is Yafforth and so they follow a signpost and are soon walking along country lanes. The heavy rain shower passes after about fifteen minutes and they stop, so James and Mick can dry their glasses; sunglasses as far as Mick is concerned.

"Well, the forecast suggested sunshine for most of the next two days," he says in response to Mick's Filey remark.

"At least we're not likely to encounter any lakes for you to dive into this time," says Andy, quickly adding, "are we, James?"

"Some splendid rivers and some large pudd—" An

oncoming car is about to drive through a puddle that covers half the road just ahead of them. "Look out!"

They all stop and turn away from the spray as it cascades towards them.

"Bloody road hog!" exclaims Andy.

"I'm not sure he had much choice," says Mick.

"Didn't expect to see three hikers in the road when he came round the bend, anyway," says James.

"How long before we're off roads and on footpaths?" says Mick.

It is unusual for him not to be in shorts and sandals at the start of a walk.

As if he is reading their thoughts, Mick volunteers, "No more rain is forecast, so I'll change into my shorts and sandals at the first opportunity."

The road bends round and past the entrance to the Romanby Golf and Country Club and then alongside it for a while. This prompts Mick to ask Andy whether he is still playing golf. He had joined a local golf club and was playing a round once a fortnight, last time they met.

"I have played little recently. I'll probably not renew my membership when it runs out in a couple of months. It'll save me a few quid. Gerry and Tom, who I used to mainly play with, aren't going as much either these days."

There is a junction ahead and James asserts, "Should be the road to Yafforth if I'm not mistaken."

He isn't, and they turn left along the B6271, signposted to Yafforth.

"Not lost your touch then," says Andy.

"There was a sign that told us that 200 metres back,"

131

Mick is quick to point out.

They pass a home furniture shop and cross a roundabout and just before the village, a garden centre and a caravan park.

"You still got that caravan you bought and towed back from Wales?" asks James.

"No, we haven't had that since last year," responds Andy. "We did tow it halfway across Europe, though. Had a great three weeks. Even Melissa enjoyed towing it."

"Wasn't it mainly Spain and France you got to?" says Mick.

"That's right. Never thought Melissa would want to share any of the driving, but to be fair, she did okay."

* * *

Yafforth is a pretty little village and several of the gardens are full of spring colour, with daffodils, fritillaries and blue grape hyacinths prominent. Though the rain has stopped, it is still cool and Mick hasn't yet donned shorts and sandals. After leaving the village, they follow the road round a large bend and then about a quarter of a mile further on James announces they must take the next right, which is signposted to an equestrian centre. They are now following a single-track road and twice before they reach the centre, they must step onto the verge, tight to a hedge to facilitate the safe passage of a 4x4 pulling a box trailer and a rather splendidly designed horsebox.

"Looks more salubrious than the camper van I used to have," says James.

A Very Alternative Coast to Coast

It isn't long before they can see horseboxes and trailers galore in fields to their right and one with an array of fences set out. A horse and rider are jumping and in the next field, several horses are being schooled or being led to or from their boxes. Some are being exercised to their left and at a couple of spots there are crossing places as horses dissect the track they are on.

"It's a real gymkhana," says Andy.

Once the sights, sounds and smells of the equestrian centre are left behind, somewhere to answer calls of nature become a priority for both James and Mick. A gap to the left bounded by a hedge and a tumbledown garage provides the ideal opportunity for both to relieve themselves and for Mick to finally change into his shorts and sandals. Andy has slowly sauntered ahead, but then decides he could do with the toilet too and he finds a suitable tree to duck behind. This whole manoeuvre eats up about ten minutes.

"Feel better for that?" enquires Andy, adding, "I see you used the opportunity to change, Mick."

* * *

They re-join a more obvious metalled road, with the occasional property on either side, before turning left along another single-track road signposted to Little Langton.

"A far cry from some of our earlier moorland and fell side route-finding," says Andy.

"Indeed," says Mick. He is secretly enjoying the virtually risk-free elements of their morning walk. "We've only had the spray from a car to dodge so far."

"I'm sure James will have some obscure detour up his sleeve to change that," says Andy.

"Ha bloody ha, I'm sure," he responds.

Mick is enjoying the morning banter with his two walking friends and now he has donned his shorts, the sun has responded by putting in an appearance. Sunglasses are flipped down from the top of his head to cover his eyes as the few houses that make up the hamlet of Little Langton are passed. Just beyond it, a deer is spotted in fields to the left and a bird of prey, probably a falcon, takes off from a tree and soars skywards, before swooping back to earth way over to the right.

"How close do we go to the actual Coast to Coast, James?" asks Mick.

"We'll be on it twice for a few miles. The first time should be soon after Great Langton, which is where we are headed next."

"Might there be anywhere there we could stop?" says Andy. "It can't be far off lunch time."

"If there is, we'll stop," agrees James.

He is feeling relaxed. The only tension today was breaking the news about their backwards route. Now that hurdle is out of the way, he can enjoy the whole day's walk, with no time pressures. They can take it easy and still be in Richmond by teatime.

Arriving at a T-junction, they bear left (the B6271 again). A hen suddenly appears and chases them until they are clear of the field she came from. They can see houses ahead. Great Langton, they discover, is probably larger than Yafforth, although shops are in short supply. They are almost out of the village altogether, before Mick spots a bench on the left, just big enough to accommodate the three of them.

"Lunch stop," he announces.

As they offload rucksacks to rummage inside for their food, before settling down to eat, Mick can sense James is getting more and more agitated.

"I thought you said we could relax and take our time today? You're not stressing about how long we're going to stop for lunch, are you?"

"No, I can't find my cap. It isn't in any of the rucksack pockets. Can either of you remember when I last had it?"

"You had it on your head when we left the station," says Andy.

"And when we all had to dodge the spray of that car," adds Mick.

"I think I took it off and had it in my hand for a while," says James. "I was sure I had put it in my rucksack."

"Have you looked thoroughly in every compartment? Take stuff out and pass it across so you can get right to the bottom."

James does as Mick asks, but no flat cap emerges.

"Bugger, damn and blast. Sally will kill me. She raised her eyebrows when I bought it because of the cost. But she had to agree it did suit, and I'd been looking for a waterproof hat for ages."

"Are you sure you put it in your rucksack?" says Andy.

"Not anymore. The only thing I can think of is I must have dropped it when we stopped for a toilet break. I certainly wasn't holding it in my hand."

"Probably not," says Mick.

"That's a good two miles back, isn't it?" says Andy.

"Nearer to three," says James.

He immediately regrets verbalising this information and might have persuaded them all to backtrack to the place they stopped if he'd claimed it was much less than two miles. He can't justify a two-hour detour to find his missing cap, even if there aren't time pressures today.

"Ah well, Sally and I are coming up to a garden centre in the area next weekend. I'll have to find a ruse to do a detour to see if I can locate it."

"It'll have gone by then," says Mick, "a quality hat like that."

"Do you mind if I eat my sandwiches?" says Andy. "We've been here fifteen minutes and I haven't eaten a bloody thing yet."

They share a laugh and focus on lunch. James is still inwardly seething and cursing his own stupidity and carelessness. He is also working on how he will avoid having to tell Sally about the cap.

CHAPTER FOURTEEN

After their lunch stop, Mick and Andy pack up their rucksacks in silence, as if starting any conversation might lead to a reference to the cap. James, of course, is lost in his own thoughts.

Finally, it is he who breaks the silence. "Right then, in about a mile, we should get reacquainted with the genuine C2C again."

He steps behind Mick to help adjust the straps on his rucksack and beams at Andy. Outwardly, he's forgotten about the cap. Inwardly, its loss is still hurting. The road rises now as it leads out of Great Langton, before levelling out again. They can see long distances in all directions and continue along the B6271. James shows where the C2C branches off to the right to head towards Danby Wiske. The route westwards to Richmond continues along the road at this point and they pass by Kipling Park and Kipling Hall to their left. They have some wonderful views of the river Swale too, as it runs almost parallel to the road along this stretch. There are some patches where the yellow gorse is in full bloom and glistens in the sunlight.

"Brilliant countryside, James, but do we get off the road soon? I feel as though I'm on first-name terms with the B6271," says Andy.

"We'll be leaving it soon and cutting across towards the Catterick garrison. Then, beyond that, we've the A1(M) to negotiate. After, it should be mainly off-road tracks until Richmond."

"It was a bit more of a challenge route-planning for this section. There aren't as many foot-paths or tracks we can take."

It is a further mile along the B6271 before they can leave it and head towards Ellerton, past a farm shop and round by a lake, towards another caravan park. The route then takes them back to the B6271, but they immediately leave to head down another track past the Bolton on Swale Nature Reserve and another man-made lake. Their path then forces them to follow the track round to the right to join again the B6271 to circumnavigate the Catterick Garrison complex. Arriving at a bridge, they spot three life-sized metal cut out sculptures of armed personnel (from the two great wars and of more recent times). The sculptures form a tableau. Andy links arms with one, whilst they take a photograph of a now four figured tableau.

"Did you know this was here, or is it just happenchance?" he asks, impressed.

"Well…" starts James.

"Did he bloody hell!" blurts out Mick, before he can add anything further.

"Well," continues James, "I knew it was hereabouts, but not that we would go straight past it."

He knew nothing about it, but he doesn't want to let his mantle as supreme guide and navigator slip as far as Andy is concerned. Mick knows him only too well.

They climb some steps onto the bridge behind the statue and turn left. The route James planned to take drops the other side of the bridge and continues along the valley bottom. When they get to this point, this path is cordoned off, and a detour is indicated by keeping straight on. They follow this for a further half a mile and still find no way to cross the A1(M), which is barring them from continuing westwards and taking them due south instead. Mick can see James getting more and more agitated because he is no longer in control of their route. Even Andy can sense James's unease.

"Shall we stop and take stock before we go any further?" It is Mick, as usual, whose intervention brings an opportunity to reflect on what the next step should be.

There appears to be a roundabout about a quarter of a mile ahead and they agree they will walk on to see whether that offers an opportunity to head towards Richmond. If not, they will return to the bridge they crossed. Mick is sure they could have passed under it and carried on in the right direction. At the roundabout, they are offered opportunities to walk down onto the A1(M) or head back to Catterick.

"It wouldn't be a challenge walk if we didn't get lost at least once on each stage," says Andy.

"We're not lost," asserts James, "just trying to compensate for an unforeseen detour. They seem to forget about the needs of ramblers in these matters."

* * *

Arriving back at the bridge, they trudge back down the steps, say hello again to the three metal soldiers, and walk beyond them and under the bridge itself. There is a track, which shortly afterwards has a fork up a hill to the left. The way ahead looks to be overgrown.

"Left it is then," says Andy, and they head uphill and arrive at a cluster of derelict farm buildings.

They can see no track coming from the left, but there appears to be a clear path heading westwards.

"Back on the right path then," says Mick.

It annoys James he hadn't spotted the way under the bridge himself.

It isn't long before they are in touch with the river again and admiring the views. It has greyed over a little; the sun having disappeared behind a band of cloud.

They can see the village of Brompton on Swale across the river and a signpost tells them they are on the official C2C again as they head towards Colburn. Their route skirts the village and they arrive at a metalled road and turn right before the pretty hamlet of Hipswell. It has a pub that does B&B and might be a good place to stay if any C2C walkers wanted to avoid the county town of Richmond. As if to prove the point barely 100metres beyond it, they meet a couple who are walking the coast to coast and are booked in the B&B tonight. They exchange greetings. This is their tenth day walking, and they reckon they have another three before Ravenscar.

James explains the route and context of the alternative C2C, but then, realising the complexities of trying to convey this, simply says, "we're walking it the other way."

"It's nice to meet other aficionados of the C2C," says Andy.

"Indeed," says Mick.

* * *

"Only about another four miles to Richmond," says James.

It is now a quarter to four. They should be there by a quarter past five, thinks James. He had originally considered they would arrive there at 4pm. The route now takes them across fields and along a line of trees before emerging at a junction of tracks. The main track veers left to stay close to the river. A less distinct track heads in the opposite direction, as if doubling back on themselves. According to the map James is using, there should be a path that crosses the river and goes through the Brompton on Swale Caravan Park to arrive on a road. Here they can bear left to Easby Abbey and then only have a short stretch to Richmond.

Bearing left along the river at the junction may be about half a mile further. Mick is keen to stick to the clearer path. Andy wants to go to the right. James tries to seek consensus and Mick gives ground. They head off eastwards along the river and can soon see the caravan park on the other side. The path they are on remains clear enough until it suddenly heads for the river, but then stops before it gets there. There isn't a passable ford and certainly not a bridge. They all accept they must turn back and head to the junction of paths. Mick is inwardly fuming they didn't listen earlier. James is annoyed about the map being wrong.

Andy inadvertently compounds matters by asking jocularly, "Which bloody idiot suggested we head this way?"

"Well, it certainly wasn't me," says Mick.

"You agreed to it. We all did," says James.

"Only after you two suggested coming this way," responds Mick.

An uneasy silence descends over them along the next stretch, and they are all walking in single file about two metres apart—James ahead and Mick bringing up the rear.

They can now clearly see Easby Abbey across the river.

James can't resist commenting, "We'd only be half an hour away from the centre of Richmond if we were at the Abbey."

Despite being at the back, Mick hears the remark. "We're bloody not, though, are we? So why bloody mention it?"

Andy considers interjecting but keeps quiet. It's very rare there is a falling out between them and if there is, it is usually quickly forgotten. He isn't used to walking in strained silence and can't remember any previous disagreement having as long an impact as this one.

They carry on walking in silence and are clearly now following the route of an old railway line. Both Mick and Andy imagine James will have been aware of this and ordinarily would relate a historical fact or two to impress them with his research. James, however, remains silent.

They see the outskirts of Richmond ahead, but on the other side of the river.

James finally breaks the silence. "There should be a road bridge ahead for us to cross and head up into the town. Might be something to interest you, Mick, before we get there."

Sure enough, a small football stadium home of Richmond Town Football Club is suddenly ahead on the left.

"What league do they play in?" asks Andy.

"Believe it or not, they play in the first division of the Wearside Football League," responds James. "The ground is called Earls Orchard."

"Anything else you can tell us about them?" asks Mick.

"They play in all blue."

"Get away with yer, man," says Andy, in his best Geordie accent. "Do you know what shade of blue?"

At this, they all laugh and the frostiness that's pervaded since the detour to the non-existent crossing place goes. The sun is out too as they cross the bridge, where they have an excellent view of the rather splendid remains of Richmond Castle. From here, they head up into the market town and locate the King's Head Hotel at the far side of the market square.

* * *

After checking in, they are shown to their rooms and agree to meet downstairs in fifteen minutes for a stroll around the town to identify any hostelries or restaurants that may be open.

Back down on the ground floor, they all study the menu for what's on offer this evening.

"There's one or two things I could fancy," says Mick.

143

"A couple of veggie options as well," says Andy.

They go out into the sunshine and turn left, spot a Chinese that has eat-in and takeaway options and a couple of pubs that have bar meals, but a lot of the cafes and restaurants apparently don't open on a Sunday night. Having covered all sides of the square and the two sides of the buildings that run down the middle of it from about halfway, they return to the King's Head.

"I haven't really seen anything better than what's on offer here," says Andy.

Mick and James agree staying put will be the best option.

"Shall we have a drink now before going up to get showered and changed and meet back here at 7.30pm?" says James.

It is, by this time, a quarter to seven. James insists he get the first round in and they sit in the lounge area, to both enjoy their drinks and reflect on the day's walk.

Despite the two-mile period of hard silence, the lost cap and the time they spent on roads, certainly for the earlier part of the day's walk, they all agree it has been an enjoyable day. The highlight for Andy has been the metalled soldier sculptures. For Mick, it is some of the river stretches and for James, teasing them about his knowledge of Richmond Town FC. He doesn't verbalise this though, instead he reflects on the horses, show jumpers, hunters and ponies they encountered—something that was completely unexpected and yet for around ten minutes had provided sights, smells, colours and spectacle to entertain. He also feels they have covered, including detours, around eighteen miles today. This was rather more than the twelve to fourteen miles he had expected.

* * *

After showering and changing, they are back down at 7.30pm and luckily there is one table still available. They hadn't thought they would need to book, but the restaurant at the hotel is packed to the gills.

"Obviously the go-to place on a Sunday night in Richmond," says Mick.

The food is good and after a second beer, the three relax into the evening and conversation turns to events at work and home. Andy updates them on the latest cutbacks, redundancies and preposterous proposals he thinks are in the offing. James reflects on how little he thinks about work, when he is away from it these days. It's only when he and Mick meet up with Andy work matters get raised. Mick listens intently to Andy's reprise of their workplace and only asks questions when he judges Andy is running out of steam.

"So, Melissa's got a place at college then. Is she going to be doing the course at York I mentioned to you before?" says James, as if to move the conversation on from work.

"Yes, she is," responds Andy. "She is really looking forward to it."

James knows Sally and Melissa have had several conversations about Occupational Therapy both as a profession and a career. Prior to these, Sally had limited contact with Melissa; the two have developed a friendship since the first contact.

It surprised him a couple of months back when Sally said to him, "Melissa's not quite how I imagined her to be from the way you described her."

He tried to revisit in his head all the feedback he gave from both his own experience and from things Andy told him, to work out what impression he gave Sally.

"She seemed chipper when Louise and I bumped into her in Booth's a couple of months ago, when on the spur of the moment we decided we'd go there for a change to do our shopping," said Mick.

A party of seven or eight men are dining at a nearby table and as the evening wears on, the laughter and banter from their table gets ever louder. They discern the group are a golfing party, who have come away for the weekend for a round of golf and to make the most of their evening together.

It is wonderful for Andy to be having conversations about Melissa and not be worrying their relationship is in difficulties. Beers have been replaced by wine now and after pudding and coffees, they all adjourn to the lounge bar again for a whisky before heading off to bed.

"So, what's the plan for the morning then?" says Andy

"The buses back from Reeth to Richmond are at one forty-five and four forty-five," Andy says. "If we get to Reeth by 3pm-ish, we could have a good hour and a half in the Overton House cafe, if that's what we want to do."

"Sounds good to me," says Andy.

"How long is the walk?" asks Mick.

"About twelve miles, so between four and five hours at most, depending how fast we want to walk," says James. "Mostly farm tracks, paths through fields and some stretches along the river, apart from the first bit hardly any roads at all."

"Suits me," says Andy.

The three of them head up to bed.

CHAPTER FIFTEEN

Louise is the first to arrive. She's known Sally for as long as Mick has known James and they have shared childcare, holidays, recipes, knitting patterns, meals together and some shared interests in dancing, music and gardening.

"Am I the first? Do you think Melissa will come?" These are her opening remarks as Sally opens the door to let her in.

"Nice to see you. Of course she'll come. She's dropping Millie off with her parents and Claire's going to a friend's."

"I've only met her twice, once at the supermarket and once when Andy invited Mick and I to watch the Tour de France, as it passed right by their house."

"Yes, I remember that. I think I had something else on, but I'm sure James went as well."

"Did he? I don't remember seeing him there."

"Oh well, maybe he just talked about going."

Sally is racking her brains to recall whether James set off to go to Andy and Melissa's. She has a splendid memory and seems certain he not only did, but he talked about it on his return. She'll have to find some way of bringing up the subject on his return.

"Anyway, sit down. I'll pop the kettle on. I've made some shortbreads and a lemon drizzle cake."

"Mmm, yummy," is Louise's response.

The two of them sit at the table in the large kitchen

diner and catch up on their own news around family and grandchildren, whilst they await Melissa's arrival. It was Sally's idea to arrange this little gathering. Since speaking to Melissa about Occupational Therapy as a career choice, they talked about other things, too. She said, when justifying it to the other two, the three of them have been swanning off together for years. It's about time we did this. She was grateful in some ways James offered her services to Melissa in relation to discussing OT. Melissa has always been more of a mystery to both Louise and her. Most of their knowledge has been gleaned from comments made by Mick and James. Neither of them was very forthcoming.

For Sally, Melissa is not at all what she imagined. She finds her to be bright, articulate and clearly doing her best to balance work, childcare and looking after the family home. Yes, she clearly struggles with the age gap in her relationship with her husband, but apart from his paranoia, from her perspective, he could be controlling, practical, money-obsessed and not always brilliant at displaying feelings or providing emotional support.

* * *

Melissa was late setting off as Claire spent ages getting ready. Appearance meant so much to teenage girls, she remembered from her own teenage years, and whilst she understood Claire's indecisiveness, today was not the day she wanted to experience it.

"Come on, Claire, you know I'm going out and I've got to drop Millie off at your Nan and Grandad's first."

"Just coming."

She resisted responding with, "And so is Christmas." She got flustered with the children more when Andy wasn't around, and the childcare was all down to her. He is such a calming influence, and both Claire and Millie dote on him. His phlegmatic character and pragmatism do grate, particularly when she wants an emotional response and is met with a reasoned practical one. He can be so bloody frustrating.

She flops Millie in front of the TV, whilst she tries to get Claire to finish getting ready. Millie takes after her Dad and isn't a difficult child to parent.

Finally, Claire appears at the top of the stairs and carefully steps downwards, making sure she stops and looks in the hall mirror at the bottom.

"Great, you're ready at last." Turning around, she shouts, "Millie turn the TV off. We're ready to go now."

"Do I look okay, Mum?"

"Of course you do, love. Millie, did you hear me?"

By the time she has bundled the two of them in the car, she is feeling inwardly stressed. Whilst she has spoken to and met Sally a few times recently, she doesn't really know Louise. She doesn't want to be late for their little gathering. She drops Claire off at her friends.

"Bye, Mum."

"Be back home by six, as we agreed."

Claire is already at the door of her friends, adjusting

her attire after the car journey. She turns and smiles back at the car, as Melissa sets off again.

Of course, she can't just throw Millie through the door at her parents' house, even though by now she is running late. It is another twenty minutes before she is on her way. She considers stopping to ring Sally to say she won't be long, but decides any further delay is out of the question.

* * *

The lemon drizzle cake has been cut and Sally and Louise are on their second cuppa by the time Melissa arrives.

"Come in, lovely to see you. The kids will no doubt have held you up and you won't have been able to rush in and out of your parents'."

"Sorry I'm a bit late. Getting Claire to engage in second gear was the major problem. She must have tried six or seven outfits on before deciding what to wear."

"Teenage girls. Our two were just the same back in the day," adds Sally.

Louise and Mick have two daughters too, so she understands perfectly.

"Nice to meet you, Melissa. We didn't really have time to talk before and apart from that, I think we only met at Booth's."

Melissa, whilst nervous about this gathering, feels a little better both Louise and Sally understand what it's like to be living with a teenager in the house.

"What can I get you to drink, Melissa, tea, coffee?"

"Coffee please, need a caffeine fix!"

"Shall we go through to the lounge? We get the sun through there in the afternoon. You can lead the way, Louise, I'll bring coffee, cake and biscuits through on a tray."

It is, in part, a deliberate ploy on Sally's part to facilitate Louise and Melissa having some time together to chat without her being present.

"I hear you're going to be starting an Occupational Therapy course in September," is Louise's opening gambit.

"Yes, I've always wanted a proper career, and it impressed me what the OT did for my Grandma, to keep her independent at home. She's dead now." She nervously adds, "My grandma, not the OT."

Louise smiles. "I don't think such things were thought of when my parents were still alive. Most of my knowledge about Occupational Therapy has been gleaned from chatting to Sally."

"Yes, she's been brilliant at sharing with me all the ins and outs of the profession and the issues she dealt with over the years."

"She's good at helping others."

"Beautiful garden," says Melissa, looking out of the window.

"I'm sure Sally will show us round later. I've been round before, but there's always something new to see."

* * *

Sally appears with the tray at this point. "Did I hear my

name being mentioned?"

"I was just saying to Melissa I felt sure you would provide a tour of the garden later."

"Be delighted to."

"Lemon drizzle cake, Melissa?"

"I shouldn't."

"But you will."

"Go on then, just a small slice."

Sally cuts a slice she judges to be somewhere between what she would deem to be small and what she would consider being large.

"There you are. Do you want another, Louise?"

"Maybe later."

"I wonder what our three intrepid explorers are up to," asks Sally.

"Where is it they're walking today?" asks Louise.

"Reeth to Richmond," says Sally. "Living with James, you have to be prepared to hear all about the planning that goes into these things. Papers and books all over the place, so he can research snippets of information. No doubt to throw out at Mick and Andy, to impress. Honestly, he can be so boring."

"Oh, Andy thinks he's wonderful, being so knowledgeable," says Melissa.

"He can certainly organise route marches," says Louise. "I only hope today's not another one of those twenty-something-mile stretches. Mick doesn't complain, but I know he'd prefer a gentler walk these days."

"If James's calculations are accurate, and they will be, it's only around twelve miles today."

"That's a relief. I remember the first day of this so-

153

called challenge, when Andy fell and broke his wrist, clambering down Bow Fell. I'm surprised you let him back out so soon, Melissa."

"I know. James was absolutely distraught when they got back. He still beats himself up."

Louise thought of saying 'and so he bloody should' but thinks better of it.

"It was a good six months later before Andy felt confident enough to venture forth," says Melissa. "I suppose accidents happen."

"Aye, too bloody often, when the three of them get together." This time, Louise's self-restraint goes missing.

"I know Andy enjoys the opportunity to talk with them both about work. I'm afraid it's a taboo subject at home."

"You're right, Melissa, I often get James regaling me with updates after he gets back. But that's enough about those three. I believe you wanted to see the garden."

* * *

Sally gets up and ushers them through to the back door and out into the garden, her pride and joy. She delights in telling Melissa the names of different plants and explaining which like the sun, which prefers shade, and others that can tolerate a little of both. At the bottom of the garden is Sally's studio shed. She unlocks the door to her creative world. Melissa is blown away by the plastic boxes of wool, books, patterns, part-finished projects and the table and chairs, rocking chair, radio, kettle, pictures and postcards adorning the walls.

Louise has seen it all before, but she remains impressed by Sally's creative workspace, particularly her wool stash.

After their tour of the garden, they go back indoors.

Their conversation turns to family, and Louise and Sally tell Melissa about their children and grandchildren. They both believe you notice milestones more in grandchildren than you do for your own kids.

"You're just so focussed on house, work and childcare. Is that what it feels like for you, Melissa?" Sally asks.

Melissa feels comfortable being able to talk to these two women, who seem to have lots of empathy with what life is like for her right now. She doesn't feel judged. Neither does she feel she has to compete, which is often the case with the women she meets as contemporaries.

"Thank you so much for organising us getting together," says Melissa. "Life can be so hectic." She is on the verge of saying more, but doesn't.

"Well, it seems ridiculous. The three of them go off together and we never meet," says Sally.

"Perhaps we'll do it again next time they're away," says Louise, adding, "you could both come to mine."

Inwardly, Melissa panics. Whilst coming out to meet Louise and Sally has been very helpful and not nearly as stressing as she thought it might be, the thought of having to entertain them at her house is something different entirely. The cleaning and sorting out she would have to do first and the baking create a little shock wave.

Sally sees the look of panic cross Melissa's face. "Don't worry, Melissa, Louise and I can do the entertaining. We haven't got kids at home leaving their stuff everywhere."

"Anyway, I didn't envisage we would meet every time the three of them go away. It would still be nice to do so occasionally, though."

"Do I tell Mick we've got together?"

"I don't think that will be necessary. Why can't it be our little secret? I bet they've a few that don't get shared with us," says Sally. She adds, "Although, James can't really pull the wool over my eyes."

"Yes," says Louise, "and you know a thing or two about wool."

They all laugh.

"I should get back to relieve Mum and Dad of Millie and to make sure we're back home before Claire." She has really enjoyed the couple of hours they have spent together.

"Would you like to take some cake or biscuits with you? Can't have James thinking I baked for him when he gets back tomorrow."

"Er, if you're sure."

"Course I am. Apart from Claire and Millie, you can always leave some with your parents."

"Thank you very much. Nice to have met you properly, Louise."

"It's been fun. Remember, next time we do this, whenever that may be, you must meet at my house."

Melissa sets off to her parents' in as good a humour

as she has been on any of Andy's walks. She knows they have their difficulties and Andy is a worrier and seems to think because she is ten years his junior, she'll go off with a toy boy in due course, which is absolute nonsense. Today, however, she is thinking fondly of him and looking forward to seeing him when he returns home tomorrow. He'll have to do without lemon drizzle cake or shortbreads, though. She doesn't want to be answering questions about where they came from.

Louise, too, is ready to depart. She thanks Sally for the afternoon. It is four o'clock.

"I wonder where our menfolk are at this point in time?" she asks.

"Probably arrived in Richmond by now and be enjoying their first pint."

* * *

Little do either of them know up in the Dales, Mick and James are walking in silence in single file with Andy between them, and that it will be half an hour before the silence is broken.

CHAPTER SIXTEEN

The three arrive for breakfast and are shown to a table in the middle of the dining area. The golfing party are all seated at the adjacent table as last night. Mick, James and Andy can pick up snatches of their conversation, but they are thankfully not as loud as they were yesterday evening.

"Sleep well?" asks Andy, looking at Mick, but addressing both the others.

"Like a log," is Mick's response.

"Me too. What about you, Andy?"

"Yes, yes, I slept well too. Remind me again, James. What's our itinerary for today?"

"There's no rush to depart. We've probably got around twelve miles to walk from here to Reeth. There are Little White Buses back from there to Richmond at quarter to two and quarter to five. Then it's a bus to Darlington, to link up with a Leeds train," James says.

"Oh yes, I remember you told us as much last night."

The server arrives to take their orders. Full English with scrambled egg for Mick, the same with poached eggs for James, and a veggie version for Andy.

"I've been reading a bit about Richmond," says Andy. "The castle, which we had superb views of as we crossed the bridge over the Swale yesterday, has apparently been here since 1071. It was a bi-product of the Norman conquest and was built, not literally, by

Alan Rufus. According to Trip Advisor, it's the best preserved, early Norman castle in England."

"I also discovered apparently Robert Baden-Powell apparently lived there for around two and a half years until 1910, when he was in charge of the northern territorial army and before he founded the boy scouts."

Andy's recently gained knowledge about Richmond castle is interrupted by food: Andy's vegetarian option and two plates of full English, both with scrambled eggs. James explains his was with poached eggs and the server goes off to locate the right diner.

"Don't wait for me," says James. "Enjoy your meal. I'm sure mine will be along in a minute."

After the server has left the dining room, still with cooked breakfast in hand and having lastly enquired at the golfing party table, Mick overhears one golfer say to another, "Didn't you order scrambled eggs, Jim?" Whilst Mick can't see the food 'Jim' is eating, the response of, "Yes, but this is just as good," suggests he may be 'enjoying' James's breakfast!

Mick and Andy both tuck in, eating slowly, hoping James's will arrive at any moment. James is inwardly getting more and more impatient as his friends' plates empty and there is still no sign. After all, it isn't as if he doesn't like scrambled every bit as much as poached eggs. Just as both Andy and Mick are putting in the last forkfuls, the server reappears, with a freshly cooked plate of food and a disdainful look on his face, clearly believing it was James who misremembered his order.

Mick senses James's discomfiture and the server's thoughts, and in a quiet voice suggests to him, "I think maybe the gentleman at the next table may have accepted my friend's breakfast by mistake."

"No worries, sir," he says with a smile.

As he leaves the table, James explodes, "What? You knew all along and kept quiet!"

He makes as if to get up and confront the errant golfer.

"Calm down, James, I didn't know. I suspected, given an overheard snatch of conversation. However, I also suspect the server was blaming you for the mix-up, so I thought I would mention my suspicions to him. At least he can go back into the kitchen now and save his own face."

"Yes," says Andy, "and you don't want your poached eggs to go cold, do you?"

James relaxes back into his chair and smiles. "No," he says, "I bet yours were by the time you finished them, the pace you were eating."

"No matter," says Mick. "Did you discover anything else about Richmond Castle, Andy?"

"Apparently it was a great draw to artists like Turner, who painted several pictures of it."

"According to legend," says James, between mouthfuls of bacon and mushrooms, "King Arthur and his knights slept in a cave underneath the castle."

"Just finish your breakfast," says Mick.

* * *

By the time the three of them go back up to their rooms, clean their teeth, finish packing and are back down in reception to settle the bill, it is after nine o'clock.

It is cold but sunny as they leave the hotel and head back into the market square.

James has regained his composure and is keen to get today's walk up and running. He heads round the square, convinced he knows where they are going. Mick and Andy follow on with a mutually exchanged shrug of the shoulders. As they exit the square and turn right down a street, a poster on the wall proclaims, 'Richmond versus Silkworth 7pm Monday night, Admission £3.' Mick and Andy watch as after a further fifty paces, James stops, first considers, and then keeps turning the map he has in his hands.

He spins round, "Sorry," he says, "must have gone past Finkle Street."

"Finkle Street," says Mick, "I think that was the second turning we passed."

"Why didn't you tell me?" fumes James.

"I didn't know you were looking for it, did I?" says Mick.

As they get to the end of the street again and re-enter the market square, Richmond are still playing Silkworth tonight, and the price hasn't gone up.

Finkle Street is exactly where Mick thought it to be and they stride purposefully down it, and then turn on to Reeth Road and up a hill to Westfields.

"Steady on," says Andy. "I thought we had plenty of time to enjoy a more leisurely stroll today."

For the second time in fifteen minutes, James apologises. The breakfast mix-up is still gnawing at him, and he has not been fully focused on either his navigational responsibilities or providing them with his usual information stream about places of interest. The speed he has had them walking has rendered conversation difficult, too.

He turns and suggests they all look back at the buildings and rooftops of Richmond below them. He gestures at the town.

"It has Britain's oldest working theatre in its original form, The Georgian Theatre Royal, was built in 1788 and operated for sixty years before it closed down. It was reopened in the nineteen sixties and, over time, restored to its former glory and subsequently extended."

"All right clever clogs, time to carry on walking I think," says Mick, "but more slowly this time."

* * *

The three carry on up the hill and then bear left over a stile to follow paths through and along fields and farm tracks to Whitcliffe Wood. Woodpeckers, blackbirds and pheasants audibly entertain them and there are plenty of wild primroses to see.

Mick and Andy are both enjoying the tranquillity of these moments and neither is in any rush to start a conversation. James is mulling over when to break the silence with a little more about the history and architecture of Richmond. He believes the route from here to Marske should be plain sailing. A pleasant, wooded valley walk should bring them to the village in about forty minutes.

"Somewhere round here is the site of one of the

more famous historical stories associated with Richmond," says James.

It jolts both Mick and Andy out of their inner thoughts, but before either has a chance to speak, James continues.

"Robert Willance was the first mayor of Richmond, but two years before he held that office, he survived an incredible accident. It was November 1606 and Willance was out hunting on his horse when a dense mist descended and his horse became completely disorientated and bolted. With Robert clinging on for dear life, it fell 200 feet over the edge of Whitcliffe Scar, which is over there somewhere," he says, pointing over to their left. "The horse died. He survived, but badly injured his leg. With no prospect of immediate rescue, he apparently took out his hunting knife, slit open the dead horse's belly and plunged the wounded leg inside." He allows the gory details of the story to sink in.

"Charming," is the response from Andy.

Mick is still a little miffed James's intrusion has broken the splendidly conversation free moments he was enjoying.

"After they rescued him, the leg had to be amputated, but he survived and lived until 1616. It is said when he died, he was buried in the grave where his leg had been buried ten years earlier."

During James's discourse about Robert Willance, Mick and Andy are so engrossed that even after its conclusion, no words are spoken. James is feeling pleased he has re-captured his role as the narrator of curious incidents, anecdotes, and facts. He simply loves to weave such details into their journey through the landscape.

They have been following a path which seems to keep bending further to the right.

It is Mick who breaks the silence this time. "I thought you said we might pass a couple of farms before we dropped into Marske?" he asks

"We haven't deviated from the path," says James.

He stops to pour over the map and to scan the surrounding land for clues to discern their current location.

"Fascinating little snippet of information about Willance's Leap," says Andy. "I don't know how you remember all the details."

"He'd be better remembering the details of the route we're supposed to be taking, rather than trying to entertain us with local anecdotes," says Mick.

"I can only think we're on this path," says James, running his finger along the map, but not sharing it with either of his companions. "If I'm right, it continues to bear right, before straightening and dropping to a minor road, which should lead to the village."

"If you're right. And what's the plan if you're not?" says Mick.

James ignores the barb.

"He usually is," says Andy.

They follow the path, which does indeed bend further round to the right. Eventually, they reach a single-track road and turn left to follow the road into Marske.

It is, however, only when they see a signpost that

confirms Marske is one mile ahead James can completely relax again. The village itself has several large, well maintained and colourful gardens and lots of trees. Lines of immaculate limestone walls dominate it. Its church, St Edmund's, was built in the 12th century and has castellated walls. There is also the Georgian splendour of Marske Hall to behold.

"Do we just follow the road?" asks Andy.

"Yes, we keep on the road out of Marske, up the hill ahead, before bearing left across fields," says James.

"Thank god for that," says Andy, who is always happier when they are 'off-roading'.

CHAPTER SEVENTEEN

It is quite a pull out of the village and all three are sweating and puffing a bit by the time a gap in the wall and a signpost offers them sanctuary from tarmac and the risk of speeding motorists.

As they approach a further stile over a wall, a group of three walkers are heading towards them. They turn out to be C2C walkers doing it the right way. They are all booked into the King's Arms in Richmond overnight.

"If there's still a golfing party staying there, make sure one of them doesn't purloin your breakfast order," James shouts after them as they bid their farewells and head towards Marske.

"That's the first C2C walker we've encountered since yesterday near Hipswell," says Andy.

He has hardly uttered this sentence, when another walker is spotted heading towards them who also turns out to be walking the C2C. He is carrying a big rucksack and has camping gear attached to it.

It clearly impresses Andy. "You camping all the way?" he asks.

"Yes, I had my dog with me for company until Kirkby Stephen, but now there's just me. I'm Dave," is his response.

"What happened to the dog?" asks Mick, adding, "I'm Mick."

"She'd clearly had enough, so I had to ring up my

wife to come and collect her."

"Did she have to come far?" asks Andy.

"We live in Coventry," he says.

"Quite a trip for her then," says Andy.

"Yeh, meant I had to camp two nights in Kirkby Stephen and it put me a day behind schedule."

"You following the 'official' route?" asks James.

"I am and if I can get as far as Hipswell tonight, I should be back on track by Wednesday."

"She did well though, getting to Kirkby Stephen," says Mick.

"Just followed her satnav I think," he smiles, adding, "I miss her, though."

"The wife?" asks Andy.

"No, the dog."

They all laugh, and he shoulders the heavy rucksack again. They wish him luck.

"Nice bloke," says Andy.

"Understanding wife," says Mick.

"Dog did bloody well to get as far as Kirkby Stephen," says James.

More fields are crossed and then they follow a track as they head for and negotiate their way into and through the hamlet of Ellers. A dead badger is lying prostrate on the verge of their path. Andy almost steps on it and lets out a shriek. The badger is stiff and has a trickle of congealed blood on the side of its head.

"Poor thing," says Andy. "I wonder how it came to meet its end."

"Probably shot by a farmer," says Mick.

"I bloody well hope not," says Andy.

* * *

As they continue along farm tracks, away from the 'murder scene', the sandstone walls of Marrick Priory can be seen in amongst the canopy of trees to their left.

Andy starts to ask, "What's tha...?"

"That's Marrick Priory," says James. "Built in the twelfth century and for four hundred years home to a group of Benedictine nuns who chose the spot because of the beauty and solitude it offered. One of the many places that Henry VIII closed and partially destroyed."

"It looks from here to be in reasonable condition," says Mick.

"Yes, it was restored in the late sixties," says James.

"So, what is its purpose today?" asks Andy.

"An outdoor educational residential facility used by schools."

As they drop to the river again and into the line of trees, they have views across to the other bank and of the prominent tower of the former priory. All agree it is in a rather splendid location. Clearly, its restoration was well worthwhile.

They are now walking along the River Swale again. At a brief stop for a drink, Andy glances at his watch. It is just before one o'clock.

"How far are we from Reeth?" he asks.

"About a mile and a half," says James.

"Do you think we could catch the earlier bus? No point hanging round in Reeth for three hours, if we don't have to."

"I don't see why not," says James.

"I thought you were keen to enjoy the delicacies of

the Overton House Cafe?" says Mick. He was certainly keen to do that, although maybe not for three hours.

Their pace quickens along the well-trodden footpath and at half-past one, they emerge from the path onto the road on the outskirts of Reeth. The gradient of the climb into the village itself slows their pace and as they round the final bend, the little white bus is at the stop, as if to taunt them into bursting into a run. Indeed, Andy breaks into a trot, which then quickens into a stumbling sprint.

As the two of them join a slightly out of breath, Andy at the open door of the bus, the driver, the same one that picked them up the last time, beams.

"Do you three always like to run for buses? No panic, we've still got five minutes here."

Mick thinks about explaining their original plan had been to get the later bus and to enjoy the delights of the Overton House cafe, but thinks the better of commencing such a conversation. The three of them board the little bus and head for the back. They have barely got seated before the doors of the bus close and it sets off. There is only one other passenger.

"Shame we missed out on the cafe," says Mick.

"There'll be a cafe in Richmond," says James.

"Will the pastries be as nice, though?"

* * *

Soon, the bus is leaving Reeth behind, but after only a short stretch on the main road, it turns up a minor road to the left. The suspension on the bus is not great, and the driver seems intent on getting them to a cafe in

169

Richmond as soon as possible. All three are hanging onto seats and being thrown about as the twists and turns of the narrow road are negotiated. The driver is whistling a tune under his breath and is clearly enjoying the more rural route back to the metropolis of Richmond. The road they are on is pitted with potholes and they feel every single jolt.

Mick is feeling rather sickly. James can feel the colour draining from his face. Suddenly, in what seems the middle of nowhere, the bus slows and comes to a jerky stop. The other passenger gets up, tips his cap to the driver, and leaves the bus. The respite allows for the briefest of exchanges between the three.

"Didn't come this way before," says Andy.

"Am I glad about that? How much further?" asks Mick.

"Can't be more than ten minutes at this pace," says James.

The bus starts off again careering along more narrow winding roads, before they slow on the outskirts of Richmond and then almost do a lap over the cobbles and around the market square before coming to a shuddering halt at the top, on the opposite side to the King's Head.

The three stand up on wobbly pins and inch their way down the bus. Mick is so disorientated, as he is getting off, he asks the driver if he knows the number of the bus to Richmond rather than to Darlington.

The driver scans Mick's ashen face. "Bit of a bumpy ride! This is Richmond. Where you headed for?"

Mick has reached solid ground and doesn't turn to respond.

"Darlington," Andy interjects.

"They leave from this stop on the hour and the half hour."

"Thanks," says James, who is the last to disembark.

The three help each other put rucksacks back in place and then drift on to find somewhere for a cup of tea. Still disorientated, they turn a corner at the top of the square and are reminded once more that Richmond are playing Silkworth tonight. They spin round and head towards Finkle Street again.

"I seem to remember there was a cafe on the left," says Andy.

There is indeed a small cafe, but no room for them to sit down and so they head back to the market square again. Eventually, they find a suitable place right outside where the bus stopped. The chosen cafe is roomy with several smaller seating areas. It is about three-quarters full, but they find a table where they can all sit comfortably together.

"Bit of colour returning to your face, Mick," says Andy.

"I'm glad I don't have to make that journey every day," is Mick's response.

"Looks to be a reasonable selection of cakes and pastries," says James, who is also feeling less queasy than he did during the latter part of the bus journey.

"Really enjoyed the walk today, James. Thank you for the usual snippets of information and for organising it yet again. It really was an alternative coast to coast, this trip, wasn't it?"

A woman about James's age, maybe slightly

younger, who is seated at the next table, interrupts their conversation.

"You boys doing the coast to coast then?" she enquires. "I've always meant to do it. The route runs past the bottom of my garden."

"Yes," says Andy, adding, "in stages."

"So where did you start this morning, then?"

"Believe it or not, here in Richmond," says Andy.

"How can that be? You mean you've not walked anywhere today?"

"No, no, we walked to Reeth, but then caught the bus back here. We're heading home again this evening," says Andy. He sounds a little flustered.

Mick notices how much eye contact their nearby diner is giving to Andy and wonders whether this is the cause.

James steps in to explain. "Today, like yesterday, we were walking backwards, east to west, on account you can't get to Reeth by public transport on a Sunday."

"Well, that's abundantly clear then," she smiles, not taking her eyes off Andy. "I'm Lucy and although I have a place here in Richmond, I spend a fair chunk of the year in a little gite I have in rural France. Where's home for you?"

"West Yorkshire, Leeds, Bradford area," says Mick, vaguely.

"Yes," says James. "He lives in Guiseley, I live in Baildon and Andy lives in Otley." He gets a kick under the table from both Mick and Andy.

"That's a coincidence. I have a friend who is a yoga teacher like myself, who lives in Otley."

Their teas and cakes arrive at this moment and the

server needs to move things around to accommodate two slices of fruit cake and a scone with butter and jam and two pots of tea.

As she departs, Lucy also gets up to leave. "It's been nice meeting you all. Enjoy the rest of your walk."

"She certainly took a shine to you, Andy," says James.

"Yes, and you practically gave her my address."

"You were a little indiscreet," echoes Mick.

Andy and James agree the fruitcake is the best they have ever tasted and that missing out on the delights of Overton House wasn't so bad after all.

They finish their teas and Mick suggests, "James's solution of walking this stretch back to front had turned out rather well on the whole."

Andy checks his watch. "Need to ask for the bill and make tracks. It's nearly ten to four. The next bus to Darlington will be here in ten minutes."

As they are all trying to attract the server's attention to pay the bill, it surprises them to see Lucy bearing down on them.

"Glad you lot are still here," she says, and addressing Andy directly. "That's my address here in Richmond and my website details, and that's the address of my friend Hilary in Otley. You should look her up."

She hands Andy a piece of paper and departs again, leaving all three open-mouthed. The server walks past their table at that point and is gone before any of them have sufficiently regained their composure.

"You two go outside and hang on to the bus and I'll settle up," says Mick.

* * *

The bus journey to Darlington takes about half an hour, but is a lot smoother than their earlier 'bus' experience. The journey is taken up with reflections about Lucy. Andy gives the piece of paper with her details on to James.

"I don't want Melissa discovering that," he says.

He distracts himself by sorting out his rucksack. They have about a ten-minute wait at Darlington before the next train that stops at Leeds arrives.

"Weren't you considering taking up yoga teaching as an alternative career, once the right opportunity to take early retirement came up?" asks Mick.

"You'd be able to get some really dedicated teaching from Lucy and Hilary," adds James.

"Shut up, the pair of you."

To steer the conversation away from Lucy, Andy asks, "So what's the next section, then, James?"

"Well, I'm glad you raised the subject, because there are different options, and I haven't really worked out what would work best. The first day is simple. Train back to Northallerton and then a walk to Osmotherley. However, from there it's 35 miles to Saltburn."

"35 miles!" explodes Mick.

"Hang on, I wasn't suggesting we walked all the way there on the following day."

"So, what are the options?" asks Andy.

"One is we could split that distance and walk it in two days."

"But that would mean the next trip would span three days and not two," says Mick.

"Exactly," says James. "So, another option would be to walk to Clay Bank on the second day. We'd probably have to get a taxi from there to get us back to the nearest station, though."

"So that would mean two trips, rather than one, to complete the challenge," says Andy.

"Yes, either two more trips or a three-day trip. Like I said, I'm not sure which option would work best. What do either of you think?"

"I think it may have to be two trips for me," says Andy. "I'm not sure I could justify taking two consecutive days off work. With Melissa, I mean, I don't think work would object."

"Well, as long as we're not doing 'stupid' distances, as Louise would say, I don't mind."

The train is now on the approach to Leeds station, so the three gather their stuff and get ready to get off.

"What time's your bus to Otley, Andy?" asks Mick.

"There's one from outside the station in five minutes, if I'm lucky, so I might have to make a run for it."

"Okay, well, I've enjoyed your company for the last two days. Take care," says Mick.

"Me too," says James, "I'll work on the plan and send something out. We can always meet up for a pint to hone the details."

"Great," says Andy as he dashes from the train as soon as the doors can be opened.

"I'm so glad he is not beating himself up about his

relationship with Melissa. They seem to get on better these days," says James.

"Yes, probably why he gave you custody of that note," says Mick.

"I'll keep it with one of my maps. Sally won't find it there, or I could just destroy it!"

"Hang on to it for now," says Mick.

They board their train back towards Shipley.

"Have you come up with a line about the cap, if its absence gets noticed?"

"Not really, I just won't raise it." He is also pondering whether the Hilary Lucy referred to is somebody he might have met before.

When he gets home, Sally is pleased to see him and shows some interest in the 'trip'. He tells her about the 'wrong' breakfast, their conversation with Dave, the fellow Coast to Coast walker, and their bumpy ride on the little white bus.

"How was Andy? Is he still stressing less about Melissa these days?"

"He was fine. Really enjoyed it. Looking forward to the next trip already."

"And Mick?"

"Mick was in good form, too. Apart from at the end of the ride on the little white bus."

* * *

Mick informs Louise of their walking from east to west, and how well this worked. She is more reassured by the shorter distances walked both days.

"Well, I'm glad you enjoyed yourself. Tea should be

ready in about thirty minutes, if you want to go shower and change."

In the shower, Mick is allowing his thoughts of the events of the past two days to mull over in his head. James can be an obstinate bugger, he thinks, remembering their fall out over the river crossing that never was. At other times, he's witty and generous. It is so good to see Andy in a good place about life at home and for him and Melissa to be getting along. He is already looking forward to the next time they will link up.

* * *

Melissa has driven the short distance to the bus station at Otley to collect Andy and is keen to share with him the creative things she has been doing today with Claire and Millie. Andy is just so pleased to see her and hear all is well.

"Brilliant two days," he says. "James had it all organised as usual, and Mick was his usual helpful and enigmatic self."

CHAPTER EIGHTEEN

Three months later, the three are once again meeting at Leeds Station to board the train to Northallerton. Only Mick and James met to discuss and plan for this leg of their journey. Andy had to cry off at the last minute, because Melissa was getting herself into a right tizz about starting her course.

Once they are all on the train and sitting down, it is the first question on Mick's lips.

"How are things with Melissa? She'll have been on the course for about three weeks now."

"She's finding it harder than she imagined, but is enjoying it. I think there is more theory to learn than she expected, especially in the first few weeks."

"Well, at least she's enjoying it," said Mick. "I'm sorry you weren't able to join James and I the other week."

"I hope you're okay with the itinerary for today and tomorrow," says James. "They're both shortish days."

"For us, anyway," says Mick.

"To be honest, I haven't really given it much thought. It's just nice to be getting away and linking up with the two of you."

"Glad we can be of service," says Mick.

"As usual, I just turn up and everything's organised."

"Today's walk is about eight and a half miles, so I expect we will be in Osmotherley by about 3pm," says James.

"Famous last words," says Mick.

The rest of the journey is spent catching up with Andy on what is happening at work. Andy always delights in his role as the maintainer of the golden thread of truth and gossip about colleagues, past and present, and the current issues that are being grappled with.

In no time at all, they are approaching Northallerton and are gathering rucksacks and leaving the comfort of the train.

"First job is to sort out our taxi for tomorrow," says James.

As they leave the station building, he goes over to the first cab in the rank of three. He comes back after a few minutes with a business card and an agreement they will call the taxi driver when they are within a mile of Clay Bank tomorrow.

"He reckons it will take about half an hour to get us back here and we've agreed to a fare of £30."

"Excellent," says Andy, "let's set off then."

They head out of the station forecourt and turn left and pick up South Parade, as they head into the centre of the town. Just before they turn right at a roundabout, they pass a bowling club.

"Crown green or flat," says Mick.

"Probably flat round here," says James.

They pass a library and are walking past a supermarket, when Andy suddenly exclaims, "I think I could do with topping up my food supplies. Didn't really have time to do any shopping yesterday, so had to make do with what I could find at home."

The trip to the supermarket takes fifteen minutes.

James is already feeling it was rash of him to suggest an arrival time in Osmotherley of 3pm.

Back out into the unseasonably warm sunshine, they turn right along Bullamoor Road.

"Straight road for a good few miles now," says James.

"I hope there will be some footpaths, too," says Andy.

* * *

All three are dressed in shorts, with a couple of layers up top. Their rucksacks are stuffed with warmer layers and waterproofs should these be called upon.

They pass the Friarage Hospital and the Hambleton Forum, which seems to be a theatre, cinema, sports and social club all rolled into one. They take fifty minutes to leave the town and for their road to be cutting through open fields. Just as well as James is bursting for a wee, and he uses the first hedge opening to nip behind and relieve himself.

"Boy, I needed that."

"Yes, we could tell," says Mick.

The road climbs gently to a rise ahead, where they find Hill View and The Byre, a former farm and stable block by the look of them. They can now see the ridge of the North York Moors ahead in the distance.

"Is that our route for tomorrow?" asks Mick.

"Yes. We should come to a crossroads soon," says James. "There should be a pub there."

It is 11.30 and Andy suggests, "maybe we should call in for a swift one. We're not in a hurry, are we,

James?"

The three debate whether a drink stop is desired. "It doesn't have to be an alcoholic beverage," says Andy.

In the event the Fox and Hounds doesn't open until twelve on a Sunday and all agree waiting around for half an hour is not an option. James is secretly relieved about this. The last thing he wants is another 'unscheduled' stop that will impinge on their arrival time.

They pass a sign to Sowerby under Cotcliffe to their right and this sparks a brief conversation about the origins of place names and which place stands out most from their time on this challenge to date. Just past Oak Tree Farm their conversation is halted as out of nowhere they spot a small complex of converted wooden shacks and barns to the right that amongst other things contain, the 'Fighting Fit Boxing Academy', 'Painting Pottery Yard' and 'Holmes Away from Homes'.

"I assume that's a cattery or something similar," says Andy.

He is getting rather bored with walking on metalled roads and is desperate to find a footpath. Almost simultaneously, he spots a footpath sign.

"Are we able to leave the road for a change?" he asks hopefully.

The sign is beside a splendid house, which, given the grounds it sits within, is aptly named Greenacres.

"Not yet," says James. "It's on the wrong side and we've probably still the best part of another half a mile to go before we take our first footpath of the day."

A little further on, and after a house in a dip

surrounded by trees, a second footpath sign appears, this time on the left.

"Is this the one?" asks Andy.

"Patience," says James. "I'll let you know when we get to the right path. Not long now."

They pass a second right turn, which is also heading towards Sowerby under Cotcliffe. A clear bridleway sign to the left shows a path to Sigston Castle.

This time it is Mick who is the first to enquire, "This the one, James?"

"No, but it's definitely the next one, about three hundred metres further on. The road bends sharp right and our path goes left into that wood over there." He points to a wooded area that runs along a hill and then down to a valley below.

"I wouldn't have minded seeing a castle," says Andy. "Today's walk's not been our most interesting stretch to date."

"Actually, you wouldn't be able to see the castle anyway, as it doesn't exist anymore. The field behind the hedgerow is the site of the former castle. It should be dome-shaped with a central mound. Below it used to be a moated enclosure. The hedge is probably where part of the moat was. When it was still standing, it was apparently a quadrangular, fortified residence."

"I see you've been swotting again," says Mick.

"Well, it's about time we came across something for James to crow about," says Andy.

"It's registered as the site of a scheduled monument of historic importance. They usually built northern quadrangular fortified castles in a symmetrical form with a central. It's not there!" exclaims James.

"I know, you said," says Mick.

"No, the footpath, there's no sign of it."

They reach a significant bend to the right in the road and James is alternating between poring over the map and searching the hedgerow to the left.

"I'm absolutely certain this is where there should be a footpath bearing left to take us into the woods."

He proffers the map to Mick with his finger, showing where he believes they are and the clearly marked footpath.

"How old's the map?" asks Andy. "Does it have a castle on it, too?"

After a short confabulation, they turn around and head back to the Public Bridleway sign to Slingsby Castle, James having confirmed they should be able to follow footpaths to regain his 'planned' route. He is inwardly fuming at being let down by an out-of-date map again.

They go through a gate and initially are still on a metalled track and can see a farm ahead. Just before the farm, there are two footpath signs. One shows carrying on through the farm and the second suggests a right turn along a public bridleway.

"Which way now?" asks Andy.

"According to the map, the bridleway should bring us alongside the wood and then after about 400 metres there should be a path down through it."

"Should, being the operative word," says Mick.

* * *

As they set off along the tractor worn track that dips

down to follow the contours that edge the field, a rather splendid old ash tree stands proudly to their left, long wizened branches sweeping down around it to form a skirt of leaves.

"Magnificent tree," says Andy, "might have had a view of a castle in its youth."

Their route does for a short while, drop low enough and arc round and could be the remnants of part of the ancient moat. A male pheasant suddenly takes off and scuttles about four feet off the ground in an arc to find sanctuary on what would have been the castle side of the moat. A few steps further on and his mate breaks cover and scuds across to join him. The bridleway now turns left and climbs the edge of the field past a gate until a second gate leads them into the next field. Ahead, they can see both cows and sheep and they stick to the path which runs close to the hedge on their right. As they near the cows, several raise their heads and look at the intruders. One turns and moves towards them, followed by a second, which breaks into a run.

"Time to leave," says James.

"Bloody hell," says Andy.

They run back to the gate without a backward glance until all three have clambered back over.

"What now?" asks a rather out of breath Mick.

"I suppose we can either go back to the road and see if there is another footpath we can take, or we can climb over the gate into the next field and walk up that to the wood," says James.

"You mean go off piste again," says Mick.

Andy is not keen to return to the road, having finally been able to leave tarmac. "I think we should try the next field. We can walk along by the hedge, so we only have that between us and the actual path."

Andy and James climb over the gate, and Mick reluctantly follows suit. "This may be a mistake," is all he can muster by protest.

They follow the edge of the ploughed field and eventually reach the top corner, which is bounded by the field with the cows and sheep and ahead by the start of the woodland. They carry straight on and are now working their way through a tangle of undergrowth, nettles, fallen branches, ivy, and other vegetation. Trying to walk in a straight line is impossible. Low-hanging branches must be circumnavigated. After ten minutes, they seem to have made little headway. Occasionally, there is a short stretch that is relatively clear, but then they are knee deep again. To make matters worse, all are wearing shorts.

"If we just try to keep going straight, we should hit the footpath, which should run down from our left," says James.

He had a nasty experience with a cow on a previous walk and has no regrets about leaving the bridleway. However, he is cursing the farmer for causing him to have to drag Mick and Andy off the beaten track again. He knows both Louise and Sally would berate him if they only knew. If Andy hadn't been so against returning to the road, he might have allowed Mick to persuade him to see common sense.

"Should hit the path anytime now," he shouts, as much to distract him from his inner thoughts as to instil any hope this might be the case.

They have been staggering through the wood for about half an hour before Mick finally explodes. "This is madness," he says, "we're no nearer to finding a way out of this blasted wood and my legs are getting scratched to bloody ribbons."

"It looks pretty hopeless, just stumbling on like this," says Andy.

"You're both right, of course," says James. "We should have come to that path by now… if it exists! How about we head up the slope to our left and try to get out of the wood and walk beside it? After all, we must be well past the field with the cows by now."

"Sounds a plan," says Andy.

"Anything's better than just blindly carrying on," says Mick.

They work their way up the slope and eventually scramble out of the wood into an open field and, as a bonus, there is a clear path for them to follow. Before carrying on, they each take a swig of water and use a few drops of it with some tissues James provides to clean muddy and scratched legs. He also digs out some antiseptic cream from his first aid kit to smear over the worst of the scratches.

"All shipshape and ready to roll?" asks James.

He has consulted his maps and asserts the area to their right is Foxton Wood and that they must have negotiated completely the Skigston Castle plantation.

"Maybe from here to Osmotherley with no more surprises would be good," says Mick. "Something to be said for walking on roads," he mutters.

"Where's your sense of adventure, Mick?" says Andy. Then, changing his tone, he asks, "What is the plan from here, James?"

"If we keep on this track, it should bring us almost to the main A684, but we'll take a sharp right and drop to a ford, where we should pick up a footpath to the left. We'll then be back on the route I had planned for us to walk."

Peter Kay

CHAPTER NINETEEN

The three soon fall into a steady pace and before long, they can make out the occasional top of a lorry over a hedge ahead, that signifies traffic on the road. They can also make out some farm buildings, which they have to negotiate a way through before they emerge on to a metalled road again. Fifty yards to their left is the main road, but they bear right and drop steeply down the single-track road. Infuriatingly, they pass a gap in the hedge to their right, which, had it been spotted before they arrived at the farm, would have saved them some time, and avoided them having to negotiate a way through it.

"Must be nearly lunchtime," says Andy. They have been walking for almost two and a half hours.

"Hopefully, there will be a suitable spot between here and before we cross the A684," says James.

"I thought we came this way to avoid it?" says Mick.

"To avoid walking along it," says James, "but we will need to cross it before we head eastwards towards Mount Grace Priory. Osmotherley is, I reckon, less than a mile from there."

They pass a house on a bend and then spot a ford ahead, which takes the road towards a farm. A footpath sign just before it directs them to walk along the banks of a brook, with a field of sheep to their left. Thankfully, there are no cows. To the right of the ford is also a footpath sign, which is where they should have emerged from the wood had they ever found a path. A look along the line of the supposed footpath would suggest it may have been several years since anyone has ventured along it.

Keeping the brook to their right gives them a clear path to follow, and the 'music' of the water helps to soothe a little. About a quarter of a mile along from the footpath sign, they find a perfect picnic spot, where each can sit on a flat rock by the water. As they wrest their pack lunches from rucksacks, even Mick relaxes. It is exactly one o'clock.

A ping on Andy's phone breaks the sound of their munching and the burbling of the water.

"Melissa" he says.

On previous walks, contact from Melissa was a sure sign something was amiss—a call he came to dread. However, recently their relationship, or rather his stressing less about it, has been more positive and such contact during one of their walks has been rare.

The call doesn't last long and Mick and James hear Andy say, "I'm sure she won't mind," followed by, "Okay, I'll ask him and then ring you back, love."

He finishes the call and turns to James. "Melissa's still getting her knickers in a twist about the theory side of the course. She was wondering whether Sally was likely to be at home and if you thought she would mind her ringing again for some advice, because she so values the help and support Sally has given her. She doesn't want to become a nuisance, though."

"I'm sure Sally would be delighted to talk her through stuff. As far as I am aware, she's no plans for the rest of the day. I know she was going to do some shopping this morning."

Andy smiles and rings Melissa back and suggests ringing Sally is fine and she should be at home.

"I remember," says Mick, "when a phone call from Melissa would set you back for an hour."

"Yes, I'm not really sure why she didn't just ring Sally. The two of them have spoken a few times already over the past few months. Sometimes she struggles with her self-confidence."

No-one seems in a hurry to depart their lunch-stop. Each flicks a picnic remnant—a crisp, bread crust, apple core—into the water and watches the item get caught by the current and float gently downstream. After a slow start, the apple core fares best and forges ahead, much to Andy's delight.

"Small things," says Mick.

"Time to make a move," says James.

"It's been one of the best lunch stops of the challenge," says Andy.

"Pity about what came before," says Mick.

* * *

Their path now crosses fields, never straying far from the line of the watercourse, until finally they must climb a gate to join a metalled road again. It brings them to the main road, the A684, where a signpost proclaims 'Northallerton 4¾ miles to the left and Ellerbeck ½ mile to the right'. James reckons they have walked six and a quarter miles to get here. They cross once the road is clear and continue along a minor road ahead. The views of the ridge walk they will cover tomorrow are clear over to their right. About half a mile along the minor road, and before a junction to the left, signposted to West Hartley, James suddenly stops by a gate to their right.

"I don't believe it," he says. "There should be a footpath running eastwards from here. There is no signpost and little evidence of any footpath either."

He is scanning the map earnestly and points out where they are, to both Andy and Mick.

There is a minor road to the right about two hundred metres further on, which might be an option, but it isn't clear whether this road would get them to and safely across the busy A19. They could carry on for another half a mile to East Hartley, where a B road should provide a more reliable route over the A19, but that would add at least another two to three miles to the day's walk. There is a pub there though, which might both provide refreshment and directions. The third alternative is to head back to the busy A684 and simply walk along that for an hour until they reach Osmotherley. Each has a different preferred option, but after debate, they agree to take the right turn just ahead.

"It should bring us out somewhere near Mount Grace Priory," says James. "I'm not sure whether we could visit the house, as it's an English Heritage site, but the grounds and gardens should be open and the footpath we want circumnavigates the house, before heading on to Osmotherley."

"So, what's the history of the Priory?" asks Andy.

"Carthusian monks founded it in the 14th Century," says James. "They lived very much as religious hermits. There were only around ten such places in the country and Mount Grace Priory is by far the best and most extensive set of remains that still exist. It is said to possess a proper sense of peaceful solitude and its location was what drew the monks there. Monks lived there only for around 150 years, before, like lots of other similar places, it was forced to close under Henry VIII's dissolution of the monasteries."

"Impressive research, as always," says Andy.

They reach the turn off by this point and head eastwards along a single-track road, with rabbits tumbling and bobbing out from the grassy bank to their right to a plethora of burrows that line the foot of the hedgerow to their left. As there aren't any squashed rabbits on the tarmac, they can only presume this is a seldom used road.

"This could be a road to nowhere," says Andy.

"Or the road to hell," says Mick.

They have walked almost a mile along it when a car approaches from behind and they all tuck into the side to let it pass. It has tinted windows and the number-plate is so encrusted with mud as to be undecipherable.

"If you saw that on a street back home, you'd probably think drug deliveries," says Mick.

About half a mile further on and they can glimpse traffic rushing past the end of their road and as they emerge from the overhanging hedgerows, the dual carriageway of the A19 stretches right and left as far as the eye can see. They can see, however, on the other side of the road a road-sign which proclaims 'Mount Grace Priory 200 metres ahead'. Keeping as far into the banking on the grass verge as they can, they edge along with vehicles hurtling towards them at seventy miles an hour. There is a break in the central reservation barrier ahead, to allow vehicles travelling northwards to turn across oncoming traffic and up the road towards the Priory.

As soon as it is safe to do so, they move across to the grass verge of the central reservation to draw level with the opening and as soon as the coast is clear sprint across to head up the side road to Mount Grace.

"That was scary," says Andy.

"We must be bloody mad," says Mick. "For God's sake, don't either of you mention the fact we crossed the A19 when you get home. I don't want the third degree from Louise."

They pass an extensive but empty and boarded up farm complex before the entrance to the grounds and the renovated Priory are reached. They can either head right through the car park, or go straight ahead up the drive and choose the latter.

"It looks in much better nick than I was expecting from your description, James," says Andy.

"Well, I think English Heritage has spent money on restoring aspects of it and added a visitor centre, cafe and gift shop," says Mick, adding, "from what I understand."

"I guess both you and I have flashed past it many times on our way up to the North East," says James, addressing Mick. Both have family just north of Newcastle.

They bear right and skirt the building, but can see no sign of any footpath. A member of staff is walking towards them and James asks if she is aware of a path to circumnavigate the priory. They are headed to

Osmotherley.

She points along the line of a ditch in a field that rises to the edge of the woodland behind the priory and rather curtly responds.

"I believe there is a stile in the fence up there."

They head up the slope to a line of fencing and sure enough find a stile. Once over it, a path heads left for four metres before turning sharp right and in a further four metres they arrive at a further stile. No human has crossed this stile for a long time and beyond it lies a tangle of vegetation and brambles.

"Blast and bugger," exclaims James.

"Do you think she knew?" asks Andy.

"Of course she did," says Mick.

* * *

Sally puts the telephone down and moves across the kitchen to switch the kettle on. She has just finished a lengthy conversation with Melissa. They have talked through the study of anatomy, physiology, ergonomics and rehabilitation. She has enjoyed remembering and sharing the aspects of being an OT that she most enjoyed and what drew her into the profession. She assured Melissa much of the role is about listening and observing in order to understand the issues facing the person you are working with.

Melissa seemed to become less anxious as they talked, and the conversation finished with her reassuring Sally she was feeling much more positive about things. The two also agreed next time the 'mighty explorers' were away, they would get together with Louise and have another proper 'catch up'.

She even found out during their 'chat' James had been at the Tour De France party, but she thought he had gone into Otley soon after the primary group of cyclists had gone past. This might explain why Louise hadn't seen him, but why hadn't James mentioned going into Otley.

The mystery, if it ever had been one, is partially, but not completely, resolved.

* * *

The three make their way down the field and can see a couple of blokes working in the garden.

"Excuse me," says James, "we're looking for the footpath to Osmotherley?"

"A member of staff sent us up to a stile at the back," adds Andy, "but it was impassable."

The chap nearest to them leans on his fork, looks up and smiles. "Aye," he says, "be a Carthusian monk what last used that theer path."

His fellow gardener laughs, but helpfully points to the bottom of the car park and informs them, "You'll find a pretty clear path to Osmotherley down there on the left."

They offer their thanks and head down to where a signpost suggests they mount another stile. At first, the path meanders along beside a fence and a ditch and then suddenly cuts upwards through the woods. The path is steep and as the three ascend further, conversation is suspended for a while. Finally, they emerge from the evergreen woodland over another stile into a field. The brightest sunshine of the day so far greets their arrival, although they must carry on climbing up the slope along the line of a hedge. They look to be heading for a farm ahead, where the prospect of a farm track beneath their feet awaits. So fixed are they on this they almost miss a footpath sign to their right.

"Hang on," says Mick, "aren't we meant to go this way?"

"Good spot," says Andy.

"Yes, well done that man," says James, annoyed he missed the way again.

Their path now levels off as they head for another farm and emerge from this onto a metalled road again.

"Quite a pull up through those woods," says Mick.

"Enough to give a man a real thirst," says Andy.

"We should be in Osmotherley in ten minutes," says James. "Just enough time to check in at the Queen Catherine before we have a pint in each of the other two pubs in the village.

CHAPTER TWENTY

The Queen Catherine has been refurbished since the last time the three stayed there, during their Cleveland Way adventures. They had all previously considered it the poshest of the three pubs in the village.

Andy soaks up the décor of the place as they check in. "Excellent make over," he says. "I thought it was really grand the last time we were here."

"I bet the Lion still has the best beer, though," says James.

"Well, let's take our stuff up to the rooms and find out," says Mick.

Their rooms all display evidence of the tasteful make over undertaken and the three reconvene in reception ten minutes later. Mick has asked for and been given the menu for tonight.

After studying it intently, he suggests, "Great choice of food here, three veggie options for you, Andy."

"Do you want a drink here before we visit the other two pubs? We can sit on the picnic benches outside," says Andy.

"Okay, I'll get them," says James, before Mick considers and responds to Andy's question.

He is still ruminating on several of the menu options for the evening and cogitating on what he should go for. Whilst James is at the bar, Andy rings Melissa and discovers she has had an extremely useful conversation with Sally and is feeling less stressed about her course.

James emerges with a silver tray on which are perched three pint-glasses filled with a golden amber coloured beer, the odd bubble gently rising and a quarter inch of froth topping off all three.

"I think you'll all like this one. I was encouraged to sample all three hand-pulled beers before choosing it."

"I thought you were taking your time," says Mick.

"Just spoken to Melissa," says Andy. "Sally did a brilliant job. She's sounding much more positive again."

"Great. Tell me what you think." He passes a pint to Andy and then one to Mick.

"Good," says Mick.

"Very refreshing," says Andy.

"My money's still on the beer at the Lion besting it," adds Mick.

The three sit and sip their beers and look across the street to the Lion and further right to the market cross and its stone table that sits on a slightly raised triangle of land that marks the centre of the village and the junction of three roads.

"They used to rest coffins on that stone table before carrying them up and over the moors to the sea," says James, as if reading their thoughts.

The three had once walked the Lyke Wake walk from Osmotherley to Ravenscar. It was many years ago, but they had never forgotten their traversing of that desolate route, setting off at 8pm and walking through the night before arriving at Ravenscar at 4pm the following day.

"Aye, I'm surprised our friendship survived that experience. It was a relentless boring slog," says Andy.

"And we didn't have the weight of a coffin to take our minds off the terrain," says Mick.

"The only interesting bit of it we did in pitch blackness," adds James. "At least we'll have that stretch to cover in the sunshine tomorrow."

At that moment, his mobile pings and he checks to find a message from Sally, confirming she has had a lengthy and enjoyable conversation with Melissa and she is sure she will be fine.

He smiles. "Sally says hello to the intrepid explorers," he says.

The horrors of the Lyke Wake walk are forgotten for the moment and the beers are finished and Andy and Mick head across to the Lion, whilst James returns the three empties on their silver tray to the bar at the Queen Catherine.

* * *

By the time James joins the other two, three pints have been pulled and two are in the hands of Andy and Mick.

"Cheers," says James, as he sits down to join the others. "Did you know Osmotherley has its origins in Viking times and was originally named 'Asmund's clearing'? In the early eighteen hundreds, it apparently doubled in size and had a population of around a thousand, most working in the alum and jet mines that were commonplace in the area."

"Interesting," says Andy.

"Really!" says Mick.

"It also had a weaving centre using the hydropower

of Cod Beck and what is now the Youth Hostel used to be the linen Mill. Sally and I stayed there years ago when the kids were in middle school."

"Yes, Louise and I stayed there with our two, many years ago," says Mick.

"So, what's the plan for tomorrow, then?" asks Andy.

"About eleven miles along, what I think we all agreed was the most physically taxing leg of the Cleveland Way," says James. "The weather's supposed to be fine and mainly sunny, so we should have some good views further inland, once we have got up to the ridges. About four to five hours walking, so we don't need to rush breakfast in the morning."

"Good as the last pint was, James, you've got to agree this is better," says Mick, draining the last of his beer.

"Shall we take in the Three Tuns before heading back to the Queen Catherine?" asks Andy.

"Or have another here before heading back to shower and change for dinner?" says Mick, adding, "We can always wander down to the Three Tuns after we have eaten, if we want to sample the evening air."

They agree to stay put and Andy heads to the bar.

***

Dinner is every bit as much of a culinary experience as Mick imagined. The three reflect on the day and Andy comes into his own as he updates them on the progress of a couple of former work colleagues and the current stresses he is facing at work. There is no rush to leave the table and the excellent wine Mick selects to 'accompany his venison' is enjoyed by all. Eventually, they decide sleep beckons rather more than a short evening stroll to the Three Tuns. It isn't as if they haven't been there before. By ten o'clock all have retired to their rooms, having agreed to be down for breakfast at eight.

CHAPTER TWENTY-ONE

Monday morning dawns grey with patches of blue dotted here and there. It certainly feels cooler than yesterday to James, who is first down to breakfast and steps outside to gauge the temperature and get some fresh air before breakfast. He is looking forward to the day's walk along the ridges of Faceby Bank and Carlton Bank and the climb up Hasty Bank to reach the rocky outcrop of the Wainstones. He wonders about an early detour to take in Lady Chapel. Maybe he can just tell Mick and Andy about it instead? Their route today will be entirely along the Cleveland Way, so there should be no risk of them losing their bearings. He can relax and just enjoy the walk and the company, he thinks, as he heads back into the sumptuous interior of the Queen Catherine and joins Andy and Mick in the dining room.

"Morning both," is his hearty greeting.

"Morning," says Mick.

"Been up long?" says Andy.

"Just been outside checking on the temperature and surveying the skies."

"What's the verdict?" asks the ever-attentive Andy.

"Cooler than yesterday, but no sign of rain."

There are only two other couples in the dining room. The server is very warm and polite and keen to ensure they are aware of what all the options for breakfast are before taking their orders. Andy is particularly smitten and can't resist commenting on her pleasantness.

"I thought you and Melissa were getting on really well at the moment?" is Mick's response.

He remembers a time when commenting on the beauty of another woman was said wistfully, as if he imagined Melissa had left him and he wasn't in a relationship at all.

"I am. Doesn't mean I cannot appreciate beauty in others when I see it, though."

"Wasn't Lucy, who we encountered in Richmond, beautiful?"

Yes, but that was different, wasn't it?"

"Only because she clearly found you attractive, too."

James hasn't seen this playful side of Mick on their 'challenge' walks before. Andy is sensitive to being teased with comments he is prone to make about the virtues of other women.

"Stop it you two. It's like dining with a couple of teenagers. Our breakfasts are here anyway."

The server delivers their cooked food with a beaming smile and asks if there is anything else they need before departing the room.

* * *

It is around nine thirty by the time they are all togged up, rucksacks are packed, and the bill is paid. They are in no rush to leave the comfortable surroundings of the hotel. The patches of blue have disappeared from the sky, but the clouds seem a lighter shade of grey as they start working off the excesses of both a hearty breakfast and last night's meal. At the market cross, they bear left and the road immediately climbs, as if to remind them of their culinary indulgences. After about fifteen minutes, Andy, who is in front, stops as they reach a divergence of possible routes.

"Keep left, we're skirting that hill ahead," says James, adding, "The right route takes you to Lady Chapel. There's a good viewpoint up ahead. We can stop and have a minute there."

They carry on, with the track still rising. The viewpoint provides a perfect opportunity to take a moment to contemplate the panorama. It also allows James to speak about Lady Chapel.

"The Chapel I mentioned back there was connected to Mount Grace Priory. It was apparently founded by Catherine of Aragon, Henry's first wife, which is why it was spared from destruction. The last Prior of Mount Grace lived there after the destruction of the Priory itself. Although it fell into disrepair, it was restored in the 18th century and to this day remains a popular place of pilgrimage. The connection to Catherine is probably where the hotel we stayed in last night gets its name from."

Their route now bears right and eventually levels off as they enter the higher reaches of the wood that tumbles down to the Priory and to the busy A19 below. They have been walking for about an hour as they reach a gate in the wall, on the other side of which stands a beacon. It is well remembered, as when they undertook their ill-fated Lyke Wake walk challenge, they somehow turned left towards Osmotherley, instead of bearing right, and it wasn't until they emerged from the trees, they realised their mistake.

This error had added two miles to what was already a 40-mile walk.

"Do you remember…?" says Andy.

"Let's not talk about it," Mick cuts in.

After a further fifteen minutes, they leave the woodland edge and head across more open country along Scarth Wood Moor and, for the first time today, the path heads downwards. They can see the village of Swainby a couple of miles ahead to their left. The path heads down to Scarth Nick and a set of steps cut into the hillside, before a cattle grid crossing of a minor road. It then rises again into yet more woodland. The three are now walking along a forest track, which allows them to be together rather than in single file.

"I'd forgotten just how scenic this section was," says Mick.

"Yes, I know the cliff top walking beside the North Sea was good, but I still think this stretch of the Cleveland Way is my favourite," says James.

"I assume you're not referring to the last stretch of cliff top walking," says Andy.

"It was after that when you dreamed up this challenge, wasn't it, James?"

Mick's question reminds James just how long ago that was. "I can hardly believe that was over three years ago," he says.

"So, our next two-day stint will see us complete it," says Andy. "Are we going to mark the occasion in any way?"

"What had you in mind?" asks Mick.

"Nothing specific," says Andy. "I just thought we should do something."

"Well, we can all think about the options and meet to discuss them and, of course, to plan the last two days," says James.

"Have a planning meeting, you mean," says Mick, with a wink at Andy.

"Good idea," says Andy. "I'll drink to that."

They pass a break in the trees to their left and have a fine view of Swainby and of the plain stretching westwards beyond. There are a couple of seats on which they can perch for a moment and take a swig of water. James adjusts the straps on Mick's rucksack before they get under way again, almost sliding down a steep slope which looks to have a mud pool at its base.

They ease their way across the gloopy obstacle with care. Mick's right leg, however, gives way before he has reached the safety of firmer ground, and he somehow ends up on all fours kneeling in the cloying mud and is helped up by both James and Andy. Remarkably, little of the mud has attached itself to clothing and James retrieves some wipes from his rucksack for Mick to clean up his hands and muddy knees.

"Say a prayer for me whilst you're down there," was Andy's response to Mick's sudden lurch forward and downwards. "I don't remember it being like that last time we were here," says Mick. "Are you sure we're on the right path, James?"

"I think it hadn't rained for a good while when we did this section of the Cleveland Way last time," says James, "so it was much firmer."

After Mick has cleaned himself up sufficiently to feel he can reasonably take his seat in the taxi later, the three carry on. Immediately before a farm, they turn sharp right and follow a trail that leads them to another pleasant woodland edge path. It is noon and James reckons they are about half-way along the day's trek. They leave the wood and go through a gate, across a field. A footbridge takes them over Piper Beck as they head downwards again. Emerging onto a road, they turn left before a couple of hundred metres later, crossing the road at a T-junction and heading uphill once more. Another gate leads to a right turn and a steep climb through the trees.

"I'd forgotten just how up and down this stretch was," says Mick.

"And how steep some ups are," says a rather out of breath Andy.

"Should level off again soon," says James.

CHAPTER TWENTY-TWO

At the top of the plantation, there is no respite from the uphill trail as they skirt the edge of Round Hill. Finally, the path finds a contour it likes and levels off to allow them all to recover from the exertions of the climb and appreciate the scenery again.

"The next four miles are superb walking," says James. "Faceby Bank, Carlton Bank and then about a mile before we bail out for the day, we've got the rocky outcrop of Wainstones to look forward to."

"I'm looking forward to finding somewhere to stop for lunch," says Andy.

"You can't have worked off both last night's meal and your cooked breakfast," says Mick.

"Veggie breakfasts and goat's cheese don't weigh you down as much as bacon, sausage, black pudding and venison," says Andy.

"Shall we compromise and agree to look from one o'clock onwards? I reckon if we don't find anywhere to stop before then, we might be at the Wainstones by about 1.30pm." He adds, "I know there are definitely places to picnic there."

* * *

Another descent follows before their trail climbs again, skirting Gold Hill before reaching Faceby Bank.

"Wonderful views," says Mick.

The panorama of the Cleveland plain is to their left as they walk along the escarpment edge of Faceby Bank.

"Sunshine's coming out too," says Andy, his need for sustenance temporarily forgotten.

They are all so engrossed with the westward view they are now walking alongside a feature of the Way. All, even James, had forgotten about it.

As if to confirm the point, Andy exclaims, "Look, it's that runway! Gliders, wasn't it?"

To their right is a bare and level patch of ground stripped of all vegetation, bounded by heathland, home to a glider club.

"It is a brilliant spot to take off from," says Mick.

"Not as popular as it once was because of hang gliding," says James.

He's annoyed he had forgotten about the gliding centre and, as a result, had no information about its provenance or history to share with his companions.

Their trail takes a left fork away from the runway, having run alongside it for half a mile and then arrives at an OS triangulation pillar to mark the highest point on Carlton Moor.

"1,338 feet above sea level," proclaims James. "That track you can see down there was used by the jet miners. We should be able to spot some soil heaps along the next stretch that bear evidence from their mining activity." He feels he has redeemed himself slightly with these observations.

"Another snippet of information from the Encyclopaedia James," says Andy.

James allows himself a smile. Mick is about to say

something but decides against it. Hang fire for five minutes, he thinks. The path now drops to a minor road, which they cross. There is a car park and picnic spot down to the right. They must climb a stile and head uphill again to Cringle Moor.

"Good job we've got our packed lunches today. I seem to remember you promising us a cafe hereabouts when we did the Cleveland Way," says Mick.

"That's right," says Andy. "It closed a few years before. We had to make do with energy bars and yoghurt-coated raisins, if I remember rightly."

Now it is Mick's turn to express a smile. James feels embarrassed at the memory. His redemption was short-lived.

They all settle on the steady climb to the nab that marks the high point of Cringle Moor. The view at the top is worth the effort and to cap it off, there is a stone seat, which Andy immediately proclaims is a 'glorious spot to have lunch.'

"How long before we get to the rendezvous point with our taxi back to Northallerton?" asks Mick.

James considers the map before responding. "I reckon we've covered nine of the eleven miles of today's walk. I was going to ring the taxi once we got to Wainstones if we were lunching there, but I can ring when we're ready to leave if we have our lunch here instead."

Andy is already delving into his rucksack to extricate his lunch. The others join him on the stone seat to follow suit. They also have a boundary stone for company and in the distance can make out the outline of Captain Cook's Monument on Easby Moor, some fifteen miles away.

James points this out before telling them the history of their picnic bench. "Apparently this seat was created here in memory of a guy called Alec Falconer, one member of a local rambling club, who created a long-distance walk across the North York Moors, continuing along the coast. Ironically, he died about a year before the Cleveland Way opened."

Both Andy and Mick have mouthfuls of food, so his snippet is met with grunts and a nod. He presses on, though.

"The rise to our right is Drake Howe, a Bronze Age burial mound. It is the second highest point of the Cleveland Way. There are supposed to be thousands of such mounds dotted about the Moors around here."

"Thousands?" queries Mick.

"So I've read," says James.

"Three cheers for Alec Falconer," says Andy. "Brilliant place for a lunch stop."

They sit in silence for a while, both enjoying their lunch and the view, before Mick says, "Do we have a time we need to be back at Northallerton, James?"

"Not really. Trains are about every hour to Leeds, so we've got plenty of scope."

The question reminds him he needs to ring Jim, the taxi driver he spoke to yesterday, to come and collect them from the car park at Clay Bank. He gets out his phone.

"Drat!" he says. "No bloody signal."

The other two check their phones before all admit contacting the taxi from where they are is a non-starter.

"I'm sure there will be a signal at the Wainstones, if

not before," says James.

"Famous last words," says Mick.

* * *

They set off again, each periodically checking phones for that elusive signal. Their route takes them closer to the high point of Drake Howe before a paved stone path allows them to wind steeply downwards again. They arrive at a stone wall and bear right before negotiating a gate. The way climbs again as they ascend Cold Moor, where they pass the entrance of an old jet mine and a tell-tale soil heap. Still no signal. Having reached the high point of the moor, they are once again going down.

"It's a right roller coaster this stretch," says Andy.

"Only one more climb to the Wainstones before our last descent to Clay Bank."

"What happens if we still don't have a signal by then?" queries Mick.

"Look, I made some enquiries a couple of days ago and was assured there will be a signal at the top of Wainstones," is James's curt response.

An edgy silence descends over the three as they climb up Hasty Bank to reach the rocky pinnacles and outcrops that mark out the summit of Wainstones. A myriad of paths weave between the rock formations. A couple of guys are using one of the larger buttresses to hone their rock-climbing skills.

James immediately retrieves his mobile and, with a smirk aimed at Mick, proclaims, "I have a signal."

Mick and Andy find a rock to sit astride, whilst

James keys in the numbers to speak to Jim. It is exactly 1.30pm.

"I have to admit I've enjoyed this section, although James can be a pompous arse," says Mick.

"He's usually got it sussed though," says Andy, "and he hasn't even got us lost this time."

"We were lost a few times yesterday."

"True."

"Do you really think we should mark the end of the last section?"

"Why not? It's been one of our best and, at times, strangest challenges to date."

Their ruminations are interrupted by James. "The good news is I've spoken to Jim, but he's on a fare at the moment, and unlikely to be free for an hour and a half. He's going to contact another driver to come and pick us up."

"I suppose that's a result," says Andy.

"I'll believe it when I see him," says Mick.

"What time have you arranged for the pickup?" asks Andy.

"2.30pm. It's only half an hour tops from here, so we can enjoy the views for longer before heading down."

"I think I'd rather we got there in plenty of time," says Mick.

They leave the rock climbers to their sport and enjoy the level walking along the Hasty Bank plateau, with its dramatic cliff falls to their left. At the last of the cliffs, the path follows a steep rocky descent, which requires each to concentrate on staying upright. They finally reach the Stokesley to Helmsley road and turn left, leaving the Cleveland Way behind as they head to the Clay Bank Car Park. It is 2.10pm.

"Well, we're here in good time," says Andy.

"If he gets here at 2.30pm, we should make the 3.10pm train to Leeds," says James.

They stay at the entrance to the car park to make it easier for the taxi driver to spot them. Conversation turns again to the last stretch of the challenge and what might be the best way to mark the conclusion of it.

Andy suggests, "Maybe we could arrange a meal out and invite the 'girls'?"

Mick is worried Louise might find out some things he has omitted to tell her about their journey across the north of England. "Do you think they'd all get on?"

"Why wouldn't they?" says Andy.

James isn't sure involving Sally, Louise and Melissa in their celebrations is the right thing to do either, but can't think of a good enough reason to kill the idea.

"I thought we were going to have a planning meeting to talk about the last section and what we might do to mark the end of the walk?" is the best he can come up with.

"We can all bring our suggestions to that gathering," says Mick.

James is thinking he could get some certificates printed off and get someone to be at Saltburn to meet them to present them. He thought of talking to Sally about whether she would be up for this. It might, however, prove difficult to justify one wife being there to greet them and not all three.

"It's 2.30pm," says Mick.

"Only just," says James.

"Have you got a number to ring?" says Andy.

"Only Jim's. I assume he will have given my number to the driver."

By 2.45pm, it's obvious something has gone wrong and James rings Jim again, only for the call to go to voicemail. He leaves a suitably worded message about their plight.

"All we can do is wait," he says.

"Is there anywhere we could walk to where we could catch a bus?" asks Andy.

"Great Broughton's the nearest place that may provide such an option."

"How far away?" asks Mick.

"About two and a half miles or fifty minutes walking."

"Well, we could set off to walk there and look out for a taxi if he's running late," says Mick.

He doesn't have much hope a taxi will ever arrive and at least that way, they could take control of the situation.

"Hang on a minute," says Andy. "I'll just google buses from Great Broughton to Northallerton."

"You could also check whether there's a taxi firm based there while you're at it," says Mick.

He is losing patience with James and his 'hope, wait, and see' strategy. James tries again to contact Jim, without success. He hates it when best laid plans don't work.

"There's a bus at 4.55pm," says Andy. "Should get us to Northallerton for 5.55pm. No taxis listed."

"Well, if we set off walking now, we should be in Great Broughton by 4pm," says Mick, adding, "and at Northallerton by 6pm. What times are the trains to

Leeds?" He directs the last remark to James.

"Ten past, I think. So, if the worst comes to the worst, we should all be home by about 8pm."

"And what time might we have been home had the taxi arrangement worked as planned?"

Mick doesn't wait for James to answer. "Three hours earlier, by my reckoning."

"Okay, keep your hair on," says James.

As Mick doesn't have much hair these days, he doesn't take too kindly to this response. He makes as if to cuff James round the ear, but Andy, sensing the move, steps in the way.

"Calm down you two, let's just start walking and if the taxi turns up..."

***

Their walk along the B1257 is a study in stony silence. They are more than half-way to Great Broughton before James's mobile rings.

"Hi, Jim. No, we haven't. Okay. Alright, I'll wait to hear from you. Oh, and Jim, we're walking to Great Broughton. Yes. Okay." He explains to the others Jim is free now, but he is going to ring his mate to find out what happened, where he is, and then ring back.

Mick is thinking even if the taxi turns up now, the best they can hope for is a train an hour earlier, which would get them home by 7.00pm. However, a bus ride to Northallerton will be cheaper. He doesn't feel inclined to share the £30 cost of a taxi.

"I'm happy to get the bus. By the time Jim gets here, it'll be nearly time for it to depart, anyway."

James feels a certain sense of obligation to Jim, but understands where Mick is coming from and doesn't voice descent, given his last light-hearted remark had not gone down well.

They are just passing the welcome to Great Broughton sign when James's mobile rings again.

"Hi, Jim. Really? I don't know how. No, I understand. Not your fault. Not to worry. Actually, we're at the bus stop now. Not long to wait. No, you needn't! Positive. Thank you all the same."

"Apparently, his mate's been waiting at the car park at Carlton Bank for over an hour. Jim's sure he told him Clay Bank. He offered to come and get us, but I put him off. I'll contact him when we're back up to do the last leg. He can drive us from Northallerton back to Clay Bank."

CHAPTER TWENTY-THREE

Their journey from Great Broughton goes without further hitch, although they jog part of the way from the bus terminal to the train station in Northallerton. They arrive with five minutes to spare, but by the time they negotiate the barrier and get up and on to the platform, they have less than two minutes to wait for their train to Leeds.

"Running for the train seems to be another one of our ground rules," Andy comments. He'd also dashed from the carriage at Leeds, as his bus to Otley was imminent.

Louise meets Mick and James at Guiseley station and drops James off on the way home. It is 8.10pm.

Mick desperately wants to say, "Only three hours later than we should have been."

However, that would mean revealing too much information about the circumstances of their delay. Louise will certainly not be impressed if she finds out he almost came to blows with James.

Instead, in response to her questions about their two days away, he responds with, "Splendid walk today along the Cleveland Way, with some great views and an interesting, if less spectacular walk on Sunday, with a brilliant lunch stop by a babbling brook. Great overnight stay in the Queen Catherine in Osmotherley."

She seems satisfied, so he says no more.

Melissa is still feeling buoyed by her conversation

with Sally and has had a good weekend with Claire and Millie. Andy's usual anxieties about how things will be at home, after he has been away, are therefore quickly dispelled. He tells her about the highlights of their two days, the luxuries of the Queen Catherine, the misleading information about their footpath from a woman at Mount Grace Priory and James's descriptions about its history and some of the other snippets he's fed them over the two days. He speaks of their walk into Great Broughton to catch the bus to Northallerton, as if it was always the plan.

James is keen to play back to Sally the re-walking of his favourite section of the Cleveland Way. However, his primary emphasis is to thank her again for speaking with Melissa and to confirm how much this meant, not only to her, but to Andy as well.

"Yes, she seemed much happier after our conversation. We even talked about other things as well. Claire and Millie, her parents, holiday plans."

James is unpacking his rucksack and putting things away.

"Tea will be ready in five minutes." Sensing this is as good a time as any to catch him off guard, she continues, "Melissa even told me about she and Andy hosting their Tour de France party and how much they enjoyed entertaining people, dressing up in French costume. She remembers Mick and Louise being there and you being there at the beginning, before venturing into Otley."

She leaves the hint of her question hanging as she plates up baked potatoes, broccoli, and places James's favourite braising steak casserole on a trivet on the table and removes the lid to let the aroma hit his nostrils.

James knows immediately he hasn't previously mentioned his premature departure from the Tour de France party, but isn't keen to respond to the subtle question, in particular because he spent a couple of hours talking to a yoga teacher called Hilary. Thanks to the chance meeting with Lucy, he had tracked her down, and they've met several times since.

"Oh, braising steak, my favourite. You're a star."

Sally knows she has opened a door and can now choose some other time to walk through it.

* * *

It is late November when Mick, Andy and James meet up to discuss dates for the last stretch of their coast to coast walk and to share thoughts on how best to mark the completion.

Andy initially thought a commemorative bench somewhere along the route would be a great idea, where the presence of such would have been very welcome to them. After due consideration, he dismisses the idea as too grand a gesture.

"Indeed," says Mick.

"Then I refined the thought to maybe just having a little plaque made, which we could attach to an existing bench we sat on."

"Did you have a particular bench in mind?" asks Mick.

"Well, there was the one we lunched at between Staveley and Sedbergh. You know, Mick, where I left my walking pole and James had to run back to retrieve it."

"Not the best idea to explain that as the significance for a plaque," says Mick.

"Perhaps not. Or the one we lunched at in Great Langton. Where James suddenly discovered he'd lost his favourite flat cap."

"I certainly don't want to be reminded of that," says James. He has a proposal to put before the other two, but his biding his time before suggesting it. "Had you any thoughts, Mick," he asks.

"Well, I wondered whether, instead of immediately dashing back from Saltburn, we could book a table at a restaurant there and get a later train home. I know it would mean getting home late, but you know how much we all like a good meal."

James has investigated getting scrolls created that would detail the route and the distance and the date of their completion of their 'Very Alternative Coast to Coast'. He has also given some thought as to who an appropriate person would be to present the scrolls. Jack's suggestion gives him the perfect opening.

"How about if we combine Mick's idea with my own?" He outlines his plan to the others.

"I like that idea," says Andy.

"Do we need to be presented with them?" asks Mick.

"No, but it would be a nice finishing touch, wouldn't it?"

"Have you someone in mind?" says Andy.

"Yes, but I'd rather keep it to myself until I've checked it out with them, if that's okay?"

Mick isn't sure if he can completely trust James, or

that having someone to present the scrolls is necessary, but they have accepted his main proposal and it will impress Louise his suggestion held sway.

"Glasses are nearly empty, my round," says Andy.

* * *

It is a sunny Saturday morning in late May the following year that finds the three of them yet again on the train from Leeds to Northallerton.

"You're sure Jim will be at the station to meet us?" asks Mick.

"Yes, stop fussing. I've spoken to him twice—the last time, only yesterday. He will be there."

It is not until they have departed the train and reached the car park and Jim waves to them from beside his cab that Mick can relax.

"Ye of little faith," says James.

Jim is keen to apologise again for the misunderstanding surrounding the pickup arrangements from their last trip. He is keen to quiz them about their journey to date, and James and Andy are happy to oblige with the significant details. Mick sits in silence.

"So, a bit of an alternative coast to coast," says Jim. "Not as alternative as a group of chaps from London, who I have dropped off and picked up twice over the past two years. The first time I met them, I thought there were just three. They were all about six foot three and built like tanks. They were each carrying a huge rucksack. I pretended not to see them at first, thinking I didn't want all that weight in the cab, but they wanted taking up beyond Reeth to the CB Inn."

"Ah the Charles Bathurst," says Andy, remembering their dalliance there after their challenging walk across country from the Tan Hill Inn.

"That's the one," says Jim. "A sixty quid fare wasn't to be sneezed at. Just as they were loading rucksacks and getting in, a fourth chap arrived of equal size and stature. We somehow got them all squeezed in. It turned out they started the Coast to Coast seven years before and had been coming up twice a year for a week at a time ever since. In reality, their C2C is one long pub crawl. They walk to the next pub and if it has accommodation and the food and beer are good, they'll maybe stay for a few days before moving on to the next inn. At the end of that week, they rang me for a lift back to Northallerton Station. In the week they'd walked just two miles down the valley to the Red Lion."

"Bloody hell!" exclaims Andy.

"I picked them up again a couple of months ago and took them back to the Red Lion. At the end of the week, they had only got as far as Reeth. Mind you, there are three or four pubs to sample, and plenty of accommodation options there."

"Wonder how long it will be before they get to the east coast?" asks James.

"Could be another seven years, I imagine," says Jim.

The story of the four 'man mountains', as Jim calls them, takes up most of their journey. They pull into the car-park at Clay Bank at about 10.45am. They settle up and thank Jim for his story and get themselves ready for the walk ahead, heads still reeling with the images of the pub crawlers from London.

Peter Kay

* * *

The climb out of Clay Bank and up onto the higher reaches of the North York Moors soon focuses minds on their own trail and the challenges of starting a day's walking on a steep slope. They stop several times to take a breather and enjoy the expansive views of Carlton Moor behind them. They cross a line of boundary stones as the slope eases across Urra Moor and then head on to Round Hill.

"How far today, James?" asks Andy.

"About thirteen miles, I think."

"I can't quite believe by the end of tomorrow, we will have finished our coast to coast," says Andy.

"Yes, it's been an interesting succession of journeys," says Mick. "Are you sure Melissa is okay with our Saturday and Sunday trip?"

"Absolutely. It was her idea. In some ways, it seemed a bit like an apology for being such a pain about not using the entire weekend in the past."

As they near the high point of Round Hill, James points out the triangulation pillar to the left of the path, surrounded by heather.

"It's the highest point of the Cleveland Way, probably as high as we have been since the Tan Hill. It's built on top of a bronze age burial mound."

They can see plumes of smoke in the far distance. Industrial Teeside at work. Almost opposite the Trig point is the Hand Stone, a guidepost that crudely depicts carved hands.

"Stood here since the eighteenth century," says

James.

Their trail now continues eastwards, descending towards Cockayne Head, where they will take a sharp left. To carry on would mean they were following the dreaded Lyke Wake Walk, as well as the official Coast to Coast route. They follow the track bed of the old Rosedale Ironstone Railway for a little while before their acute turn.

"We should be able to see Captain Cook's Monument and Roseberry Topping in about a mile," says James.

"Always good to know," says Andy, adding, "You weren't able to get us accommodation in Great Ayton this time, James."

"No, we're staying about a mile further on at the King's Head in Newton Under Roseberry, so it will be another steep start tomorrow," says James.

They pass another ancient way marker and a second stone, which has carvings on three sides.

"Initials of landowners and dates of boundary agreements," says James.

They pass more burial mounds, including the clearly visible Burton Howe, as well as evidence of former ironstone workings. As the lie of the land levels out, they can see Roseberry Topping. Beyond it lies the conurbation of Teesside.

"About five and a half miles covered so far," announces James.

"Nearly time for a lunch stop," says Mick.

"I'll echo that," says Andy.

"Let's look out for the next suitable spot," says James. "We've about three miles to go before Kildale and that rather nice cafe. Be a shame to delay lunch and then not have room for a cake!"

"Indeed," says Mick.

CHAPTER TWENTY-FOUR

They find some stones to sit on and fish out an assortment of goodies. The sun has rather flirted with them so far, but it puts in a timely appearance to coincide with lunch. Mick has a good cough and a few good blows on a handkerchief.

"Got a bit of chesty cold that just doesn't seem to want to budge," he explains.

"I thought you were wheezing a bit at the start," says Andy, "but then that first hill caught us all out a bit."

After their lunch break, they carry on for about half a mile to a fork in the path. James is lost in thought. He heads down the left-hand one, without really thinking about it. The others follow. Mick is not sure they are on the right track as they seem to be dropping steeply.

"Are you sure this is the right track, James?"

James stops and consults the map. "We should have taken the right fork back there. Sorry."

After a quick discussion, they agree to head to the right until they reach the correct path and wind their way across tufts of heather. Once the 'correct' path is reached, they continue first along it and then down from Battersby Moor to a cattle grid. As they drop lower, the coolish breeze lessens, as it does, the warmth of the sun seems to intensify.

***

For the rest of the of way to Kildale they are on tarmac. It means they can walk three abreast, providing a perfect opportunity for Andy to update his friends on current issues at work.

"They're planning another management shake-up. We may all have to re-apply for our jobs again."

"That's a worry. What are our chances?" asks Mick.

"Well, in each of our cases, there are three people in similar roles and only two posts in the future. You'll both be alright because of your lengths of service. My current role probably has the most vital imperatives within it, so I should be okay."

"What's the timescale?" asks James.

"Well, you know the old firm, supposed to be resolved by the 30th of June, but it'll probably be the autumn."

"Good luck to us all and let's keep each other posted," says Mick.

Andy updates them on the progress of a former colleague and, in no time at all, they are in Kildale.

The cafe is open, so they head inside to order drinks and cakes. Chocolate and pear cake for Mick, a tiffin for Andy, and a Victoria sponge for James.

"How are things with Melissa and her course?" asks Mick.

"She's still finding it hard, but she is definitely enjoying it."

"Probably less than sixteen miles to go before we get to Saltburn," says James.

"Seems a long time ago since we were at St. Bees," says Mick.

"Not as long ago as the man mountains from

London, though," says Andy.

They gather up the last crumbs of cake and finish their teas.

It is 3pm. "We should be at the King's Head by 5pm," says James.

* * *

They have another steep climb up a metalled road, before turning left into and through woodland as they ascend to the stone tower that is Captain Cook's Monument. Iron railings have now been erected around it to prevent graffiti. Roseberry Topping, the so-called Yorkshire Matterhorn, is next to be conquered, but that will have to wait until tomorrow. Mick is glad of the opportunity for a brief stop at the monument. His chest is still bothering him. The three of them continue down to the metalled road and leave the route of the Cleveland Way as they head into Great Ayton.

It is a good two-mile walk along the road; arriving in the village where they stayed last time, they struggle to pick up any signs to Newton under Roseberry.

James spots two women up ahead and hurries on to ask directions, whilst Mick attends to a loose bootlace and Andy studies the contents of an antique shop window. James is in animated conversation for a good five minutes with the two women and returns with a broad smile on his face.

"What was that all about?" asks Andy.

"They were very pleasant and were enquiring about our exploits, so naturally I filled them in with a little of our itinerary."

"I'm sure you did," says Mick.

"We must double back and take a road to our left, which was on our right just after we entered the village."

"I thought that might be it," says Andy.

James resists commenting. Mick just gives a shrug of his shoulders.

They find the route and stick to the main road as it winds northwards out of Great Ayton. The road eventually loses any semblance of footpath, and they must walk along the verge towards the oncoming traffic, which as it is nearly 5pm, is much busier than they are expecting.

The accommodation at the King's Head is well presented and comfortable and after showering and changing, they reconvene in the bar. They discuss plans for tomorrow, and Mick and Andy try to get out of James who he has arranged to present them with the completion certificates.

James is still holding out on this information and wants it to be a surprise when they get to the restaurant tomorrow evening. It will be another opportunity for them all to spend time with someone they met about fifteen months ago. A meeting which, soon afterwards, facilitated his becoming reacquainted with Hilary. Not that Mick or Andy know anything about this. Mick is still feeling uneasy about the entire presentation idea but lets the moment pass.

Talk then turns to what their next challenge walk may be.

"I think we should stick with a linear walk, which we can do in stages," says James.

That format has worked very well," says Mick.

"The two-day arrangement is great for me," says Andy, "although I think just using one of the weekend days might still be best, despite Melissa's change of heart about this trip."

"Distances should reflect the last few stretches and not see us trying to do a day one again," says Mick.

"And I suppose it needs to be near enough to facilitate us getting to and from it in reasonable time," suggests James.

"That gives you enough to go on," says Andy, directing his question at James.

"I think so."

They take their drinks through to the dining area and are shown to a table. The King's Head is obviously a popular local eating out venue.

Mick studies the menu intensely, as if searching for the 'x' on a treasure map.

"Bit peckish," he says.

After five minutes, he declares, "I can't decide between the speciality sausage casserole or the steak and ale pie."

"I was thinking of the sausage," says James. "If you get the steak and ale, I'm more than happy to share."

"It's so much easier being a veggie," says Andy, "not the same range of choices. I'm going to have the broccoli and cauliflower gratin, with roasted vegetables and creamy mashed potato."

"Oh, that sounds appealing," says Mick.

He eventually opts for the sausage casserole.

"How are Claire and Millie doing, Andy?" asks Mick.

"They're good. Claire is studying hard for her GCSEs, but she has lots of friends at school and has played hard, too. Millie has another year after this before she starts 'big' school. I get more one-to-one time with them, currently, with Melissa having to study most evenings. No, they're both good."

"I can't believe Millie is nearly at secondary school and Claire is doing GCSEs," says Mick.

"I remember Claire as a baby coming with Melissa to meet us near the end of the Lyke Wake Walk," says James.

"That was the highlight of the walk for me," adds Mick.

They all laugh. Their meals arrive and all three tuck in. James and Mick share portions as suggested, and it isn't long before all three plates are empty.

"Excellent choice," says Mick. "Thanks for the share, James. Both the sausage and the pie were delicious."

"I bet it won't stop you having a pudding, though," says Andy.

"Be churlish not to," says Mick.

"Might help with the cold," says James. "You seem a little less troubled by it since we got here."

"Yes. It's definitely climbs that affect me the most."

Mick has been struggling with it for about four weeks now and has promised Louise if it is no better after this weekend, he will ring the doctor.

"Maybe you need some antibiotics," she told him.

He was more concerned about who James has arranged to present the scrolls tomorrow. He and Andy tried several times to get a name out of him, without success. Maybe a couple of malts after the beers they've had may loosen his tongue.

Whilst he trusted James with walking arrangements, he doesn't like surprises and it is clear to him James is planning such. James can be such a smug bugger. Mick just hates being in the dark.

The pudding plates leave the table as empty as the mains and they retire to comfortable seats, nearer to the bar.

"My round," says Mick. "Care for a malt, James, or a gin, Andy?"

"Don't mind if I do," says James.

"Can I have a vodka?" says Andy. "It's fast taking over from gin as the new drink of the moment."

Mick knows for James and himself, nothing betters a neat malt whisky as an after-dinner drink.

As if to prove the point, James volunteers, "Nothing quite like a malt."

"So, what time do we need to set off in the morning, James?" asks Andy.

"I reckon it's about five hours walking, plus an hour for stops. If we left at 9.30am, we should be in Saltburn for 4pm."

"What times the meal booked for?"

"I think Mick said 6pm."

"So, we wouldn't want to get there much before 4pm then."

"Breakfast around 8am."

"Or even 8.30am."

"What's that about 8.30am?" says Mick, arriving back with their drinks.

"Breakfast in the morning," says Andy.

233

"Yes, we don't want to get to Saltburn too early and have to hang around for ages waiting for your mystery guest to appear, do we, James?"

"Worry not. There are things we can do to kill an hour in Saltburn."

Mick waits for James to take a sip or two of his malt then asks, "Do we know this mystery guest then?"

"You may do."

"Either we do, or we don't."

"You have both met her."

James knows immediately he has already given too much away and steels himself to withstand any further verbal probing from Mick.

"A-ha, it's a woman, then."

James smiles and draws a zip across his lips. Mick's mind is whirring away, conjuring up the names of all the women the three of them might know.

"Not a relative?" asks Andy.

James repeats the zipped lip manoeuvre. Andy and, in particular Mick, continue to press, but it is clear James isn't going to reveal more this evening.

They agree to meet for breakfast at 8.30am and head off to their rooms.

CHAPTER TWENTY-FIVE

Louise is busy putting the finishing touches to the salads and carefully placing her freshly baked scones on to a cooling tray. Nibbles are ready and drinks are in the fridge chilling. She surveys the scene with contentment and for the fifth time, checks the cushions and place settings on the outside picnic table and the rooms in the house that may be visited to ensure they are neat. Declaring herself fully satisfied, she pours a glass of lemonade and goes through to the lounge to await Sally and Melissa.

She is delighted to not only be hosting this afternoon's little soiree but also to finalise their plans for tomorrow. It had been a brilliant coup of hers, she thought, to get Sally and Melissa to agree to a trip up to Saltburn tomorrow to surprise the chaps and to join them at the restaurant she had recommended to Mick. She spots a car pulling up outside and gets up to go to the door.

* * *

Melissa has been really looking forward to this weekend but now it's here, she's not as excited about things. After dropping Andy off at Leeds Station, she returned home to rouse the children and try to get them to get things ready for their two-night stop over with her parents. She is picking Sally up this afternoon and then they are off to Louise's house in Guiseley. Tomorrow afternoon, they will all drive up to Saltburn to meet up with Andy, Mick and James. Sally told her Louise had waxed lyrical about the restaurant they would meet up in. She persuaded Andy to change the arrangements for this last trip to a Saturday and Sunday, so it won't affect the kids' schooling or her course. He had been reluctant to propose a change to the others at first, conscious, no doubt of the times in the past, when she had railed against him for taking two days out of the weekend to go off walking with his 'trek buddies'.

Claire is not as keen as Millie at the prospect of a weekend with grandparents. She has studying to do and would have preferred to take a break from a stint of revision by seeing one of her friends, but it's just one weekend, so she goes along with it, but clarifies it's a great sacrifice on her part. Millie knows she'll get to stay up later and have more time reading Harry Potter. Claire isn't overjoyed at the prospect of getting dropped off at school on Monday morning by her grandad. Not exactly cool, is it? Melissa is relieved when she has finally bundled the pair of them in the car and driven the fifteen miles to her parents' house.

"Thanks for this," she says, not sure whether she is directing her remarks at Claire or her parents.

Back in the car, she texts Sally to let her know she will be with her in 45 minutes.

* * *

Sally has got an assortment of cheeses and some

crackers to take to Louise's. She knows Louise planned to bake, so she had agreed to get some savoury items but still isn't sure about their Sunday trip. Gate-crashing the guys' celebratory meal seems vulgar somehow. She certainly wouldn't have approved of it had it been she who had arranged a meal out with two women friends, only to have the dynamics of their evening changed by the arrival of their partners and James.

At least with Melissa present this afternoon, she can convince Louise James was at the Tour de France party, before going into Otley. It will be a delight to scotch any apparent mystery for Louise as to why she and Mick had not seen James there. She packs up the cheeses and crackers into a cool bag as the clock approaches 2pm and Melissa's imminent arrival. She has grown quite fond of her since their shared conversations about Occupational Therapy and Melissa's career change. It's nice to feel needed by someone. James would always much rather be in the great outdoors walking than spending time with her. She still felt there was a kind of mutual love between them and shared respect, but she had to concede James wasn't one of life's great romantics.

* * *

Sally spots Melissa's car pulling up outside and gathers the cool-bag, coat and handbag together and makes for the door. Melissa is coming down the drive.

"Can I use your loo? Don't seem to have had a minute to spare since dropping Andy off this morning."

"Of course, be my guest. You know where it is."

A slightly less flustered Melissa re-emerges. "Phew, that's better!"

"Rounding up kids and getting them to move at a pace you need them too, I bet."

"Yes, Claire was in a foul mood. I'm sure she'll make us pay later, for the sacrifice she's had to make by going to her gran and grandad's."

"Ah well, you've got the rest of today and all tomorrow, child-free."

"What's Louise's place like? You made me feel very welcome when I came here last year."

"It's a large semi-detached, with a nice garden. There probably won't be a thing out of place, but just relax. Louise will enjoy entertaining us both."

As they pull up outside Louise and Mick's house, Melissa can see the curtain twitch and before she and Sally have time to get out of the car, the front door has opened and Louise is standing there with a beaming smile, waiting to usher them inside.

"There, what did I tell you? She can't wait to play hostess."

Melissa smiles, recognising Sally's description of what to expect had been spot on.

"Hi, welcome to my humble abode."

Sally smiles inwardly at the absence of any reference to it being Mick's house, too, in her introduction.

They go into the hall. Louise is in her element. "Lounge to the right, loo at the top of the stairs, but there's another as Sally knows, right at the top of the house. Dining room beyond the lounge. If it gets too cold or rains, we'll adjourn into there. However, I've set the picnic table outside for us to sit round."

"Shall I just pop the cheeses and crackers in the kitchen, Louise, or would you like me to take them straight out?"

"Just pop them down for now. Shall I put the kettle on and make some tea, or would either of you prefer coffee?"

"Coffee please," says Melissa.

"Tea for me," says Sally, adding, "something smells nice."

"Just a few scones I rustled up. We can't plan on an empty stomach."

Ten minutes later they are all sitting round the outside table, hot drinks to hand, cheese and crackers on the side and scones taking centre stage, with butter, cream and little individual pots of jam surrounding them.

"How's the course going, Melissa? Sally seems to think you are enjoying it?"

"Yes, it's really interesting, albeit challenging. Sally has been great when I've needed to chew the cud. I'm coping, though it can be stressful. I suppose I heap that on Andy. He's good at holding the fort, though, and responding to the needs of the kids."

Melissa has probably uttered more words in response to Louise's question than she did in the conversation she had with her at Sally's last year. She is already thinking she has said too much and needs to be a little more circumspect for the rest of the afternoon.

"Good to hear."

"So," says Sally, "tell us about this restaurant we're heading for tomorrow."

Melissa feels relieved the conversation has moved away from her and believes Sally has done this deliberately to turn the spotlight away from shining on her.

"It's a plush boutique hotel that has a bar and dining room and a reputation for fine dining. Mick and I had a five-course meal there to celebrate an anniversary a few years ago. They actually do a seven-course dinner, if you are starving."

"It'll be posh frocks and make up then," says Sally.

"What about the chaps?" asks Melissa.

"Oh, they won't be wearing frocks," says Sally.

"Or makeup," says Melissa with a giggle.

"I made sure Mick had an appropriate set of smart casual clothes packed carefully in the bowels of his rucksack," says Louise.

"I know James has packed some 'eating out wear', as he called it."

"I just hope Andy has something suitable, too."

"I'm not sure why they felt the need to go out for a celebratory meal in the first place," says Sally.

"I think it was James's idea to mark the occasion and Mick's suggestion they go to Brockley Hall," says Louise.

"And your suggestion we go up and join them," adds Sally.

"Well, I don't see why they should have all the fun. It'll be nice for the six of us to get together, won't it?"

"If you say so," says Sally.

"Do I detect you're not so keen, Sally? You sounded okay about the idea when I first mentioned it."

"I know. It's just a shame it breaks our cover. It would have been nice to go on meeting without them ever knowing."

"It's also a little unfair on Melissa, as she has the only vehicle that's big enough for all of us to fit in."

"I'll ask Andy to drive us all back, so I've only got to drive one way."

"Will he be alright with that?" asks Sally.

"He'd probably prefer it."

They all laugh. "More scones, anyone, or cheeses?" says Louise.

"Excellent scones, Louise, but I need a minute before another one," says Sally.

"They are absolutely scrummy," says Melissa. "The look on their faces will be something when we walk into the dining room at Brockley Hall!"

"Yes, how easy was it to upgrade the table to a six and explain the reasons it had to be kept secret from the chaps?" says Sally.

"I do always enjoy a little subterfuge," says Louise. "I explained it was a surprise party for one chap and laid it on thick. I told them the chaps thought they may have to rush their meal to catch a train, whereas we would transport them home and therefore we could stay longer to enjoy the delights of their fine menu. I let slip that Mick, who made the booking, and I had dined with them before and very much appreciated both the food and the ambience of the place."

"I bet that last bit clinched the deal, Louise, and speaking of subterfuge, you remember telling me you and Mick hadn't seen James at Melissa and Andy's Tour de France party?"

"We didn't."

"I know, but I think Melissa may throw some light on the matter." She looks towards Melissa.

"Yes, well James was there, but he left pretty early as he said he wanted to go into Otley to sample the atmosphere there. I think you and Mick only arrived about ten minutes before the first riders came through."

"So, if I was a bit taken aback when you mentioned you hadn't seen him, I've since been able to establish both with Melissa and James that he was there, but then went into Otley."

"That's all right then," says Louise. "What time do we need to set off tomorrow and where are we meeting?"

"Well, I thought it would be helpful if I drove us to Otley. We can leave my car there. That will mean neither Melissa on the way up nor Andy on the way back will have to drop either of us off."

"Sounds good," says Louise.

"Melissa and I reckon it's about a two-hour drive, so if we got to Melissa's by about 3.30pm, it would give us room to get there before 6pm. I'll aim to get here by about a quarter to three, if that's okay?"

"That should give us plenty of time," says Louise. "These scones won't keep till Monday, so now the business side of meeting up today is resolved, let's move on to other things."

* * *

A walk round the garden is agreed, the justification being that a little bit of exercise might just provide room for more of Louise's delicious home baking.

Sally is feeling pleased at having cleared the air in relation to whether James was or was not at the tour De France party. Whilst she is still somewhat annoyed at James for not having relayed the full details of his whereabouts on the day in question, she feels ninety-nine percent certain the matter has now been resolved. Maybe it will be nice for the six of them to enjoy a meal together and for them to have more such occasions in the future. After all, she and James are used to dining with Mick and Louise and she is keen to foster her burgeoning friendship with Melissa.

Melissa is feeling relieved the afternoon hasn't all been an inquisition into her newly chosen course of study and, whilst apprehensive about the two-hour drive tomorrow, feels grateful to Sally for having reduced it from being a potentially longer one.

Louise is happy her scones have turned out so well and been so warmly commented on. She is happy as well, to have been able to regale Sally and Melissa with the delights they can expect from the Brockley Hall. Her botanical knowledge is on a par with Sally's. She has also rehearsed enough information about the contents of her flower beds to provide a running commentary as she guides them around the garden.

"I suppose working part-time affords you more hours to indulge in such pleasures," suggests Melissa, conscious both Sally and Louise seem to have time a plenty to spend in their garden oases.

She has little opportunity to spend in the garden.

What little work is undertaken in the name of horticulture is most definitely Andy's domain.

* * *

Lucy is at her cottage in Richmond. Hilary should arrive within the next half an hour.

She thinks back to her meeting with James, Mick and Andy in the cafe off the square in the town and her rash act of giving Andy her address. Little did she know then what might follow because of her impulsiveness. She had been drawn to the overheard story and recollections of their walk and always wanted to walk the coast to coast. She smiles inwardly at remembering her immediate attraction to Andy. The fact he lived in Otley, where her best friend and fellow yoga teacher, Hilary lived, seemed to add to the attraction and present the possibility of being able to bump into him again.

It had come as a bit of a bolt out of the blue when, a couple of weeks after that meeting, she had been contacted by James. He explained to her how he had ended up with her address details. He had also told her of his meeting with a woman called Hilary who was a yoga teacher and who lived in Otley and how they chatted for a couple of hours and got on really well. Things happened quickly after that. She had spoken to Hilary, who confirmed James's story and had been happy to meet him again. Lucy enjoyed playing cupid, particularly as Hilary was clearly enjoying the arrangement.

Lucy had also been surprised by James's later

contact about presenting the scrolls. She had been reluctant to agree at first, but had subsequently agreed to the opportunity of a delightful meal out and another opportunity to chat to Andy. What she hadn't told James, though, was that she had invited Hilary to come. She chuckled to herself as she imagined not only Andy's face when she appeared, but James's face when he set eyes on Hilary.

She is still smiling to herself when the doorbell rings. Hilary's beaming presence fills the doorway.

"Not too early, am I?"

"Wonderful to see you. Come in."

"You look glowing as ever."

"Must be something to do with the company I was expecting."

"Why is someone else joining us?"

"Ha-ha. I'll put the kettle on. How was the journey?"

"Hassle free." She plumps herself down on Lucy's squishy and comfortable settee. "So, what time do we need to set off tomorrow for our secret rendezvous?"

"Half four, 5pm. I'll check it on Google. Plenty of time to catch up before then."

Lucy sets down the tray with tea, milk and teacups on it. "Did you want a biscuit, or are you still watching that figure of yours?"

"Well, there's only usually me to watch it, unless I'm with James, of course."

"When did you last see him?"

"Couple of weeks ago."

"He's clearly still not lost his attraction then."

"It's still exciting, but we both know it's fun. We'll enjoy it while it lasts."

"I can't wait to see his face when he sees you tomorrow."

"I'm quite looking forward to seeing his face, too."

They both laugh.

"I thought we'd eat in tonight. There's a rather nice white in the fridge and the 'booze' cupboard is well stocked."

"Sounds perfect."

CHAPTER TWENTY-SIX

They are all sitting round the breakfast table at 8.30am on the dot.

"Good night's sleep?" asks Andy.

"Yes thanks," says James.

"Woke twice with a bit of a wheezy chest," says Mick.

"It feels strange to be contemplating the last day of this challenge," says Andy. "I honestly think it's been our best walk yet."

"It's certainly had its moments," says Mick.

"I've enjoyed doing it as much as planning it," says James.

"And you've lined us up some woman to give us a scroll that'll remind us forever of the route we took," says Mick.

"Yes, I'm pleased with the way the scrolls turned out," says James, not rising to the bait.

Cooked breakfasts arrive and eating takes over from reflective conversation.

It is about 9.30am when they are departing the King's Head and heading back toward Great Ayton, looking out for a track that will take them to the zigzag of a path up Roseberry Topping. The Yorkshire Matterhorn itself is difficult to look at directly as the rising sun seems to be perched half on its summit, throwing light out in all directions. However, as they get closer to the foot of their climb, it gives more of an impression of a sunset, as the angle of their eyeline increases.

It is certainly a steep ascent, not helped by the impact of the recently eaten breakfast and their food excesses of the previous evening. For Mick, it is even more of a challenge. He is soon trailing behind the other two as they propel themselves forward up the slope. Periodically, James and Andy stop and wait for Mick to catch them up. It is usually Andy trailing in the wake of the other two, and whilst he feels a good deal of sympathy for Mick, it also pleases him he isn't bringing up the rear on this ascent. It takes three-quarters of an hour for them to be blinded by the light again, as they finally reach the summit and the trig point upon which Mick half falls, half slumps to gather his breath.

"Good cardio workout," says Andy.

Mick has already determined he will ring the doctor's tomorrow and make an appointment to get some antibiotics to shift the lingering chest infection, which has made his ascent so arduous. On one side of the Trig Point, someone has creatively painted an excellent likeness of Shaun the Sheep.

James voices an equally excellent take of Peter Sallis speaking as 'Wallace' to Shaun.

"There. Nothing to fret over. Just a quick shampoo. We've tested this on Gromit. Haven't we lad?"

Andy laughs out loud and even Mick manages a smile.

"Did you know that image was there and spend time practising those lines?" asks Andy.

"I'd absolutely no idea," says James, with a hint of a

twinkle.

They linger at the summit long enough for Mick to recover before heading downwards with the land stretching away and into the distance, where it appears to be falling into the sea. The sun is now high above them and is painting the landscape they are heading to with vivid colour.

To their left, they have the industrial conurbations of Middlesbrough and Teesside. To their right, Captain Cook's Monument and their route of yesterday and to the west a vast plain that stretches as far as the higher Dales and the north Pennines.

"Great long-distance views," says Andy.

"I take it there are no more climbs like that?" asks Mick.

"Should be plain sailing from here," says James.

"Now where have I heard that before?" says Mick.

They arrive at the right angle of a junction of fences, at which point their route re-joins the Cleveland Way again.

They have lost sight of the sea for now, but a wonderful open panorama lies ahead. They cross Newton Moor, heading for the corner of a forestry plantation.

"Apart from the second day when we set off in light rain and mist, we've done okay for weather, haven't we," says Andy.

"The ascent of Nine Standard Riggs was tricky with the force of the wind," says Mick.

"And the first hour of the Northallerton to Richmond leg was wet," adds James.

"Overall, we've done, okay," says a slightly

chastened Andy.

They go through a gate in the forest fence and head to the right. They follow a track that skirts the plantation, then a wide track that takes them up onto Hutton Moor, before heading left to Black Nab, a small hill, but large enough to cause Mick to struggle a little with his chest infection.

"You are going to ring the doctor tomorrow and try to get something to help shift that, aren't you Mick?" James asks.

"I am, even it means acknowledging Louise was right in suggesting I should have done so two weeks ago."

"It seems worse today than yesterday," says Andy.

"Didn't have a sheer ascent of Roseberry Topping to contend with at the start of the day," says Mick.

They follow a stone wall along a clear path, with views down into and over the woods. Soon after passing the access point to Highcliffe Farm, the ground rises again to a viewpoint: Highcliff Nab. From here they can clearly see the town of Guisborough below. The path now plunges them into the woods and for the next two miles, they have the joy of working out the correct route, as there are a myriad of different paths running in all directions. The signage along the Cleveland Way is, however, good and James seems to have memorised the route from their last visit along this stretch, as he confidently strides forwards. They encounter several pairs and one larger group of cyclists, either heading towards them or cutting across their path. A disused quarry provides a great place for cyclocross, judging by the number of tyre tracks that bound up and down the undulations flowing in and out of the quarry clearing.

Suddenly, Andy and James realise Mick, who was behind them, is no longer in view and they stop to allow him to catch up.

Just when Andy suggests, "We should go back and make sure he's okay," Mick appears.

"Pitstop for a wee and a drink of water," he tells them, adding, "I think I need to make sure I take on plenty of fluids with this damn chest."

"Good idea," says Andy.

"Once we clear these woods, we should come out on the A171, near the Fox and Hounds. We'll all be able to take on some fluids there," says James.

"I remember it," says Andy. "Great spot to stop for lunch."

"You can't be that hungry," says Mick, "and you'll need to save some room for our five-course meal tonight."

"Worry not. There'll be a good five hours in-between the Fox and Hounds and Brockley Hall."

"And another five miles of walking, too," says James.

Their wait for Mick and conversation has eaten up about ten minutes and been in the shade of the trees. James suddenly realises he is feeling cold.

"Time to get going again," he says.

He turns round so he is facing east again and is suddenly aware of a divergence of two tracks and he is no longer sure which one they should continue along. A quick scour of the map doesn't help him either, as there are lots of places where paths crisscross and go off in different directions. He hates it when other distractions upset his navigational confidence.

Andy is first to spot his hesitance. "Not lost again, are we?"

"No real sign of which route to take. I'm inclined to head down the right fork."

"How far do you reckon we are from this pub?" asks Mick.

"Probably about a mile," says James.

"Well, if we're not there in half an hour, we've taken the wrong path," says Mick in a matter-of-fact way. "Lead on."

Conversation ceases as they follow the track and have more decisions to make as their route divides several times. They search in vain for an acorn sign to signal they are on the correct route. Eventually, Andy thinks he can hear a road ahead, and he heads off to the left to see if he can establish visual contact with what they all hope is the A171. Mick and James stop and await the outcome of Andy's scouting mission.

He returns with a beaming smile. "I can see a railway line and beyond it the road, with a roundabout."

James consults the map. "Yes, I can pinpoint where you're looking. We still need to be heading right though, that roundabout is a mile and a half beyond the Hare and Hounds. We should be within half a mile of it."

Suddenly, to James's relief, they emerge onto a concrete road which drops steeply and a Cleveland Way sign stares back at them, pointing them downwards.

Another quick check of the map and he announces, "There is a stile just down on the right. Not far to go now."

Across the stile and after another five minutes, they can glimpse the road down through the trees to their left. The path seems to run parallel to it for a while as it weaves its way through the trees before they arrive at a large gate and then drop to the road. There is no footpath, and the pub is about 200 metres to their left, so they cross and walk along the overgrown grass verge until the access road to the Hare and Hounds is reached.

* * *

Lucy and Hilary have enjoyed their morning. A leisurely breakfast, a stroll round the market square and for Hilary the opportunity to browse in the antique, bric-à-brac and art and craft windows. She has even bought a watercolour she thinks will be a perfect edition to her 'therapy room'.

"Shall we go for a coffee? I'll show you the cafe where I met the chaps," says Lucy.

"Great idea. I think I'm window-shopped out, anyway."

As they sit and sip their lattes, Hilary asks, "So what exactly was it again that prompted you to accost three poor guys, who were probably all just minding their own business?"

"Well, I couldn't help but earwig their conversation and the more I surreptitiously watched, the more I fancied the older one."

Peter Kay

"Andy."

"It was only later I heard him referred to by name."

"Shame really. James said if you'd met Andy in an earlier life, he might have been more receptive to your advances. You are apparently exactly the type of woman he used to drool over. That was before he met his wife. Melissa, I think James said she's called."

"Story of my life, always finding the right man at the wrong time."

"There have been one or two wrong men at the wrong time, too."

"True."

They both laugh.

"I still have trouble imagining you and James together."

"I think cos I'm so left-field for him, it kind of brings out a passionate aspect he'd forgotten he had."

"He must bring something to the party. He's certainly livened up your sex-life over the past fifteen months."

"Well, it had been dormant for a while before him, hadn't it!"

They both laugh again.

"What time do we need to set off this afternoon?"

"4.30pm should be soon enough."

"Time for a little more sightseeing in Richmond then."

CHAPTER TWENTY-SEVEN

Mick and Andy sit outside round a picnic table, rucksacks discarded. James has gone inside to order drinks and check out the menu. They have snacks in their sacks, but 'you never know?'

"You're certainly struggling a bit with that chest infection," says Andy.

"I hope it doesn't spoil the enjoyment of our meal tonight. You know how much you like your food."

"Bit chilly sitting here. I think we might be better joining James inside."

"I agree. There's a cool breeze and we're out of the sun," says Andy.

The two go inside and join James, who is just about to leave the bar with a tray of drinks. They find a table and sit down.

"Bit too chilly out there," says Mick.

Having consulted the menu, they all order soup and a roll, as if to confirm they need something to warm them before tackling the last leg of their walk. They get into conversation with a couple of women at a nearby table and discover one of them is the mother of a professional football player, who, until the last transfer window, had played for Bradford City. She had enjoyed her trips to the area near where they all live and singled out Saltaire for special praise. He has now returned to a club in his native northeast.

Feeling rested and warm again, they head out to find

the Cleveland Way. This means a short stretch along the grass verge, before turning right uphill into a quarry. The path climbs steeply to the right, round the rim of the quarry, before it eventually levels out.

"I thought you said there were no more hills," says Mick.

"Nothing like Roseberry Topping I said. If you were in tiptop health, that last bit wouldn't have troubled you," says James.

Climbing a stile, they have another uphill track, with a wooded valley dropping steeply away to their left. Another stile at the end of this stretch takes them into a field where they bear left and the ground levels out again.

"Finally, I might walk and talk at the same time again," says a wheezing Mick.

They pass Airy Hill Farm and can see a village about half a mile away to their right.

"That's Boosbeck," says James, "and before you ask, yes, it has a pub!"

"I vaguely remember this bit," says Andy. "Don't we hit one or two villages on the way into Saltburn?"

"Skelton," says James.

"Isn't there a Skelton Green before that?" asks Mick.

James scans the map. "You're absolutely right, Mick."

It is easy walking along Airy Hill Lane and they are soon on the outskirts of Skelton Green. At a T junction, they cross over the road and squeeze through a stone stile and are walking through open fields again. A second wider stile brings them to a large stone circular seating area with good seaward views and is a perfect place for a sit, a drink of water, and another opportunity to reflect on the highlights since leaving St Bees and the next walking challenge.

"I think Sedbergh to Kirkby Stephen was my favourite stretch," says Mick.

"I enjoyed walking backwards to Reeth," says Andy.

"Difficult to choose," says James, "but getting you two to stay at the Tan Hill was special."

"The aroma of sweaty lycra-clad cyclists," says Andy.

"The spectacle of Lithuanian flame-throwers," says Mick.

"Friendly Polish chambermaids," says James, winking at Andy and adding, "Only about another hour and we'll be in Saltburn."

They tear themselves away from the calm of their viewpoint, which has sheltered them from the cool of the breeze and head into the larger town of Skelton, where the route takes them along roads, streets and avenues before they drop through an underpass and emerge on the edge of a wood, which they enter shortly afterwards. Saltburn, which had been clearly visible, is now obscured from view and it is the birds and the wind through the trees they can hear.

"We could be absolutely anywhere," says Andy.

"I remember this stretch from before," says Mick.

"Skelton Beck," says James, "runs down to the sea. I think we follow it virtually all the way."

Suddenly, the towering structure of Saltburn viaduct dominates. A Network Rail sign proclaims this is Bridge SSK1/3. It even provides a map reference NZ661202.

"There's a few times during our journey across from St Bees, a structure with a map reference might have come in handy," says Mick.

He is pleased to have completed today's walk and his chest is troubling him less. He is looking forward to their meal later this evening, and a return to the Brockley Hall.

The three of them are deliberately slowing their pace as they enjoy the peace and tranquillity of their walk down the wooded valley that encloses Skelton Beck and which provides the southernmost boundary of Saltburn.

"I think I can smell the brine of the North Sea," says Andy.

"I think I'll dip my toes in it," says Mick. "It might make up for not plunging them into the Irish Sea."

"Well, we've got plenty of time to do that," says James. "A luxury we didn't have at St. Bees."

"I can't believe that's over three years ago," says Andy.

They finally leave the sheltered greenery of the Valley Gardens and head up a path that brings them out just beyond Station Road. Instead of heading to the station, however, as they had done on their last visit, they turn right and walk the two hundred metres to the cliffs above the sea. A zigzag path takes them down to the promenade and they head towards the pier and walk to its end. It is the furthest point east they can walk.

"Did you know this is now the only remaining pier in Yorkshire?" says James. "Opened in 1869 and it's a great success."

"Fancy that," says Andy.

"The area around the mouth of Skelton Beck is where the old fishing village of Saltburn was located. Apart from the Ship Inn, a favoured hostelry for smugglers apparently, there's not much of the old village left," says James.

"I'm just glad to be here," says Mick.

They stand and watch the churning grey foaming waters below and breathe in the salt air and shake hands with each other to mark their achievement in getting to the end of their Coast-to-Coast walk. Looking back, they can see the fine stone fronted properties that seem to rest along the cliff edge and give the town an air of grandeur. Rising to meet them is the funicular lift that conveys passengers up and down from seafront to town.

"That's the oldest operating water-balanced cliff lift in the country," says James.

"Once we've dipped our toes in the sea, I suggest we take the lift to the town," says Andy.

"Sounds good to me," says Mick.

They head back along the pier before turning towards the cliffs that tower above the town to the south.

"That's the route of the Cleveland Way, isn't it?" says Andy.

"I'm glad we're not doing that today," says Mick.

The beach is a mixture of sand, pebbles and crushed shells. They stop a couple of metres from the water, take off rucksacks, remove boots and socks, and uncover their feet.

"Bloody cold," says Andy.

"Therapy for the soul," says Mick.

"Are you spelling that, S O L E," says James.

"Ha ha," says Andy.

They head back to the funicular, pay their fares, and wait to be transported up to the delights of Saltburn. It is five o'clock; they still have an hour to kill before heading to the restaurant.

* * *

Louise is ready and waiting for Melissa and Sally to arrive. She is looking forward to visiting Brockley Hall again. It had been their thirtieth wedding anniversary celebration when they dined there before, with some friends who lived in nearby Redcar. She smiles to herself as she remembers the occasion and the frock she wore, which had been a present from Mick. It had amazed her he remembered her admiring it in a boutique in Leeds. They had been on a shopping trip there. That he had gone back later and bought it for her birthday, and that it fitted her so well, had made it an extra special birthday and anniversary year.

She is brought out of her daydreaming by Sally and Melissa. She hopes for the tenth time during the day they have made the right decision about going up to join the men.

"Right then," she says to Melissa, "next stop Saltburn."

"You and I might like a little comfort break half-way up if that's okay?" says Sally, addressing Louise.

"Well, we should have time," says Louise. "We don't want to arrive before the three of them, do we?"

"I think I'd appreciate a stop, too," says Melissa. "I'm not used to driving the MPV any distance."

"What make of car is it?" asks Louise.

"A Volkswagen Touran," says Melissa. "Andy's pride and joy."

"Men and their cars," says Sally.

"We only got it because of the need to have a car big enough to pull the caravan," says Melissa. "Apparently you can configure the seating in the back to hold five adults."

"So, seven seats in all. Impressive," says Louise.

"I hope we're not going to talk about cars all the way to Saltburn," says Sally. "I can think of a thousand more interesting things to chat about. How's the course going, Melissa?"

"It's going great, thanks. Being on placement and assessing real people has been a great learning curve for me."

"Do you think we're doing the right thing, going up to join the men?" asks Louise.

"It was your idea, wasn't it?" says Sally. "If it had been up to me, we would have stayed at home and just had a get together like yesterday. I never thought it was a great idea to break our cover and reveal to the chaps we had been meeting whilst they were away playing."

"I know it was my idea. I just keep having second thoughts today. I'm sure it'll be okay. I have such fond memories of dining at the Brockley Hall with Mick and Tom and Anne."

"Who are Tom and Anne?" asks Melissa.

"I went to school with Anne and she and I have kept in touch ever since.

"You sold the restaurant so well, Louise," says Sally. "That's what swung me around to agreeing to your suggestion."

"I assume you don't want me to turn round," says Melissa.

It has been the prospect of driving the Touran for a hundred miles that has been her major worry. Once she is there and she can give the keys to Andy for the return homeward journey, she will relax and enjoy what promises to be an enjoyable night out.

"I believe it is probably one of the best places I have ever eaten," says Louise.

"Well then, what's the worry? Eating out with the three chaps, who we've probably been wedded to for the best part of a hundred years between us, can hardly be a chore, can it?"

"Do you mind them going off for chunks of time and leaving you to deal with all the domestics?" asks Melissa.

It's only two-day chunks and besides, it gives me time to myself to decide what I want to do with the day. I enjoy the freedom," says Sally.

"Well of course, you're not really a walker, are you Sally? I'd be happier to be out walking with Mick. It's something we both enjoy. We wouldn't be walking crazy distances either."

"When they started doing it, I used to get really pee'd off," says Melissa. "The kids used to play up something chronic. Claire's into her schoolwork, music and friends now and Millie can amuse herself reading books."

"It is more difficult when you still have children at

home. I think James said that's why they all agreed to only walk on one of the weekend days, so Andy could be at home with you on the other."

"Oh, I hadn't realised," says Melissa.

They leave the three lanes of the A1(M) and head along the winding slip road to the A19.

"I feel safer with two lanes," says Melissa.

"Very smooth ride so far," says Sally.

"Two lanes all the way to the outskirts of Middlesbrough from here," says Louise.

* * *

Lucy and Hilary are also on the A19 and are making good progress. They should be in Saltburn in just under an hour's time.

"So, what exactly did James say about Andy and me?"

"It was more he suggested Andy would have been more receptive to being chatted up. He clearly found you attractive though, because James said when he and Mick teased him about your interest, he got all defensive."

"Mmm, maybe I'll flutter my eyelashes again tonight, then."

"Maybe not, Lucy."

"It's alright for you, you can flutter away at James."

"You know I can't. He'd be mortified if Mick and Andy found out about us."

"Why? They're supposed to be his best friends."

"Yes, and he wants to keep it that way. He doesn't want to put them in the position of having to cover up for him."

"If you say so. It seems strange to me."

"Trust me, it would be better all-round if the only people who knew about me and James were the two of us and him."

"It'll be fun to see the look on his face tonight, though."

"It will, and the look on Andy's."

CHAPTER TWENTY-EIGHT

The funicular takes less than a minute to carry them up to cliff tops, where there is still plenty of evidence of the Victorian grandeur of Saltburn's heyday.

"It was one of the most popular seaside resorts for many affluent Victorians from across the north-east of England," says James.

"Aye, you can tell from the architecture, a lot of it was built in Victorian times," says Andy.

"Saxon invaders gave it its name, 'Seatt-Burna' meaning salty stream."

"Well, let's just have a gentle wander, to soak in its atmosphere. I suggest we get to the restaurant about fifteen minutes beforehand," says Mick.

"Give us time to get changed and freshen up for our guest of honour," says Andy. "What did you say she was called again?"

"I didn't. Just wait and see."

"I hope all this Secret Service stuff is going to be worth it," says Mick.

James just smiles. Mick is getting increasingly hacked off by James's cloak and dagger routine.

They have headed north along Marine Parade and now cut up towards the station along Diamond Street. All the streets are named after precious gemstones, amber, pearl, emerald, garnet, coral, ruby and diamond. At the station, they head back south towards Valley Gardens, before turning along Glenside, which overlooks the greenery of the woodland they'd walked through about an hour ago.

"It's even grander than I remember it," says Mick, as they arrive at the entrance to Brockley Hall.

"Perhaps we should have found somewhere to change before we got here," says Andy.

"No, it's okay. I explained when I booked the table, we would need to get here a little early in order to change from our walking gear into evening wear."

Mick leads the way. They are warmly greeted and shown through to the gentleman's cloakroom. A small nearby room has been made available for them to change.

It is still only 5.50pm when they head back into the main reception/bar area.

"Celebratory drink, gents," offers the barman, who has clearly been briefed on the story behind their dining at The Brockley this evening.

"Your table is all ready, Mr Horrocks, if you would like to follow me."

The server places their three pints on a silver tray and leads them through into the restaurant.

"It's weird hearing your Sunday name, Mick," says Andy.

"Well, it is Sunday," says Mick.

James has arranged for Lucy to text him when she arrives so he can meet her in the reception area. They are shown to a large table, which appears to be set for eight.

"Are you sure this is right?" asks James.

"Positive," he responds, with a smile.

Before any of them can question him further, he

turns to leave. "Back in a moment with your menus for the evening, sirs."

At that moment, James's mobile pings to show an incoming message. He glances at it and sees that Lucy has arrived. She is just parking up and will be in reception in two minutes. He excuses himself on the pretext of needing the loo.

"I'll check on the table situation at reception, whilst I'm away," he says.

Andy is drinking in the décor and glitz around him. "I can see why we needed to pack evening wear. If the food's anything like as good as the surroundings, it's going to be an epicurean delight."

As if to emphasise the point, the server returns with their menus and both Mick and Andy scan them with anticipation.

* * *

Hilary drives into the Brockley Hall car park. She is pleased she has found the place without a hitch, thanks to her SatNav and Lucy's reassurances she was on the right roads.

"Well, we're here. What next?"

"I'll just text James to tell him we've arrived and maybe give him a minute or two before I go in. You'd better stay in the car for a little longer. I'll text you when it's safe to come and join us."

"Are you sure this is a good idea?"

"Bit late to back out now," says Lucy, pressing send on her phone.

"Might need to use the facilities before joining the

267

chaps. Check hair and make-up."

"You look fine, but I agree. I'll make an excuse to come back to reception once we're at the table and text you. I'll have worked out where the ladies are by then."

"Good plan."

They watch as a large black car pulls into the car park and three women get out and walk up to the entrance of the hotel and disappear inside.

"Fifties, sixties?" suggests Hilary.

"What! Oh, the ages of those three. I suppose so. Hard to tell when us women put on our finery. I'm sure we could pass for forties in certain company."

"Well, I certainly feel younger at the moment," says Hilary.

"You said you'd had the same effect on James."

They both laugh.

"I'd better meet him then."

* * *

James enters reception at the very moment Sally, Louise and Melissa do.

"Surprise, surprise," mouths Sally.

"Wow... What... Well, I never." He walks towards them and guides them over to a table by the bar.

"We came up to share the celebrations with you three," says Louise. "Where's Mick?"

"Mick and Andy are just getting changed. I'm the advance party just getting in drinks. Speaking of which, what can I get you three?"

"A glass of white wine would be nice," says Louise.

"I'll have my usual. No, I'll have a glass of white

wine, too," says Sally.

"Better just have a lime and lemonade," says Melissa. "Need to make sure Andy's happy to drive us all home before I have an alcoholic drink."

"You've all driven up then?" asks James.

"Melissa's driven us up in Andy's pride and joy. There's room for us all to fit in it," says Sally.

"So, the three of you won't have to dash off as early to catch a train," says Louise.

"I'll go get the drinks," says James.

He walks over to the bar and sends a quick text to Lucy, suggesting she hold fire. He'll be out to meet her in a couple of minutes. He quickly explains the predicament to the barman and asks if there is any way another table for six can be provided in the second dining room of the hotel. The barman agrees to speak to the duty manager. He comes through a couple of minutes later to talk to James, whilst the barman pours the drinks. He quickly understands the situation and agrees to James's request.

"Give me five minutes to get a table ready and I'll come and take you through. We weren't planning to use the breakfast room this evening, but it is just as pleasant as the main restaurant."

The server is prepared to bring their drinks across, but James says he would rather make a couple of trips.

"More thinking time," he winks at the barman.

After James has delivered drinks to the girls, he makes an excuse to find out what's taking Mick and Andy so long.

As he turns the corner, Lucy is walking towards him. "I thought I…"

"Listen, it's cold out there. Is something wrong?"

"No, no, just needed to check on something. Mick and Andy are through here."

He guides Lucy into the restaurant, without being seen by the wives. His head is hurting from trying to work out how the hell he is going to keep Lucy and the three wives apart. Andy spots him and Lucy first and lets out a kind of hysterical, 'Ohhh'. Mick turns in the direction that Andy's frightened gaze is fixed on.

"So that's who you organised, is it? No bloody wonder you wanted to keep it a secret. No offence, Lucy, but James should not have sprung such a surprise on us."

"Thanks for the welcome, guys. I was thinking he'd stood me up. It took him so long to respond to my text telling him I had arrived."

"My apologies, Lucy, there was an extremely pressing matter I had to attend to. Speaking of which, I wonder whether you and Mick would hold the fort. I need to have an urgent private word with Andy."

"Everything alright?" asks a bemused but slightly relieved Andy as he stands up and follows James.

"Don't be too long," says Mick.

"He seems rather jumpy tonight," says Lucy.

Once out of earshot, James quickly appraises Andy that their wives have arrived to surprise them. He's sorted a table for six in a different dining area. He now needs Andy to hold the fort with Melissa, Sally and Louise, whilst he goes back to rescue Mick and somehow keep Lucy happy.

"Couldn't she just join us? You can explain... On second thoughts, maybe not."

"I'll think of something."

"We were thinking you'd got lost, or found some other company to dine with," says Sally.

"Hi, darling," says Melissa, addressing Andy.

"What a nice surprise," he responds.

"Where the hell is Mick?" asks Louise. "He's not had a fall or something similar to what befell Andy, has he?"

"Mick is a little under the weather," says James. "Chest infection's been bothering him, but you'll be pleased to know he is phoning the doctor tomorrow to see about some meds to help clear it. He said he regrets not following your advice sooner."

"I expect he does. So, what's he doing, having a lie down somewhere?"

James spots the Duty Manager coming towards them.

"Let's sit down at our table and I'll fetch him. I'm sure your presence will buck him up to no end."

"Not off again are you, James? I've barely seen you since we all arrived," says Sally.

"Won't be long."

CHAPTER TWENTY-NINE

As the three girls sit down with Andy and the server presents them with their menus, Melissa wastes no time in asking Andy if he would mind terribly driving them all home later.

"I drove up in the Touran, so we could all be together in the one car and have room for us all on the return journey."

"Bloody hell," says Andy. "You've only ever driven it as far as your parents and back before. You got here in one piece?"

"Melissa did a brilliant job with the driving," says Sally.

"I'd be more than happy to drive us all back again," says Andy, knowing he'll be a nervous wreck with Melissa driving.

He is also relieved to be where he is and not in the other dining room with Lucy and Mick. He wonders how the hell they're going to keep Lucy apart from Melissa, Sally and Louise.

* * *

Mick has to admit Lucy is an interesting woman. They have discussed menu options, the wine that should be ordered and Lucy's gite in France and what she most enjoys doing when she's out there. Mick has described some highlights for him in the last few sections of their walk. It surprises him to discover she once walked the Lyke Wake walk and seemed to get some enjoyment out of it. She walked it with a friend.

Lucy finds Mick rather tedious. His recounting of their walk over the past few days, particularly so. She is not surprised he, James and Andy had walked the Lyke Wake walk, but disappointed Mick was so damning of it.

"What the hell was so important that required Andy to be dragged away? I might have teased him a little when I first met you chaps, but I don't bite, you know."

"He's finally got his head round the fact he has a positive relationship with his wife after stressing about her leaving him for many years. He doesn't want to jeopardise that. James must have known inviting you to join us this evening might be scary for him, the amount of teasing you laid on him when we met you in that cafe."

"So, you don't think James should have invited me?"

"I don't think it was the best plan he's ever hatched."

A ping is heard and Lucy excuses herself to scan the message from Hilary. 'What the hell's going on? Where are you? I'm coming in.'

"Apologies. I need to pop out to reception to make a quick phone call. You know what I want to drink if the server returns. Back in a mo."

* * *

As James re-enters the reception area, he heads straight for the bar.

Peter Kay

"How's it going, sir?"

"So far, so good. Thanks for your help and for getting the Duty Manager to see me so quickly. Can I have a Talisker please?"

"Certainly. Do you want ice with that, sir?"

"Just as it comes. Need a bit of thinking time."

"I can imagine."

James takes a sip of his whisky and as he does so, he spots Lucy leaving the restaurant and heading towards the entrance door. He downs the whisky and makes after her.

"Lucy!"

She turns in the lobby way and waits for him to catch up. "Where the hell have you been and where the fuck is Andy?"

"I can explain."

The hotel door bursts open, in walks Hilary.

"What the...?" says James.

"Probably my turn to explain," says Lucy.

"I thought you were going to come out to meet me and we were just going to surprise him," says Hilary, adding, "Hi gorgeous," to James.

"I didn't really want to come on my own and who better to bring with me than Hilary? I thought it might please you to see her, too."

"In normal circumstances, I'd be absolutely delighted."

"What do you mean 'normal' circumstances?" says Lucy.

"Mick and Andy don't know about Hilary. I'd rather keep it that way. So, bringing my beautiful paramour to sit beside me for two hours and for me to pretend I

274

don't know her is hardly normal, is it?"

"I told you he wouldn't want Mick and Andy to be in the picture, didn't I," says Hilary.

"However," she adds, turning to James, "if you can bear it, the plan is after our wonderful meal, I drive to Richmond, drop off Lucy, then I drive you all back to Otley, Baildon and Guiseley. If I drop you off last, we can have a little time together at the end of the evening."

The three have moved back into the main reception area and James knows acutely he has not yet delivered Mick to the second dining room and Andy has been on his own with the three wives for the past five minutes.

"Shall we just sit down at the table and try to explain things without the detail of Hilary and I?" says James.

He steers the two of them into the restaurant, where they join a rather quizzical Mick.

"Who's this? Where's Andy? What the dickens is going on, James?"

It is the perfect line for James. "Would you two ladies mind if I just took Mick into reception and explained things to him? I don't want him losing his cool and getting us thrown out."

"What do you mean, losing my cool?" says Mick, rising from the table, mumbling an apology to Lucy and Hilary.

"By the way, this is my best friend, Hilary," says Lucy, before they depart.

* * *

Sally is growing impatient at the prolonged absence of

James, and Louise is worrying about Mick. Three times one or the other has made to get up and go look for the pair, only for Andy to come up with some reason why it might be best to leave well alone and to reassure they will join them any minute now.

Sally has had enough. "No more prevaricating, Andy. I am going to find them." She rises from the table and heads to the door into reception.

"I'll come with you," says Louise.

"I'd rather you stayed with Melissa and Andy. I'm sure Mick is fine."

"It is 6.15pm," says Melissa, "I thought we were supposed to be dining at 6pm."

"We haven't been able to order anything as yet. The server won't come in until we're all seated. I've seen him hovering twice at the door," says Louise, upset at the firmness of Sally's request for her to stay put.

* * *

James just about has time to get out the words, "Our wives are here," before Mick spots Sally heading towards them.

"I've secreted them away in…"

Mick butts in, "Hi, Sally. James was just telling me you were here."

"I heard something about secreting us away. What the hell is going on, you two? We've been waiting for nearly ten minutes. The server's been hovering to take our order for ages. For god's sake, come and sit down. This was supposed to be a celebratory meal, wasn't it?"

"Oh, hi, love, yes, sorry, just wanted to make sure

Mick was feeling up to it. He struggled a bit with his chest today."

"I'm fine, really. Stop fussing. Let's just sit down, as Sally suggests."

They go through to join the other three.

"At last," says Louise. "How's the chest, Mick? We all thought you two had got lost." She gets up to give Mick a hug and they all sit down.

"Right, first things first," says Sally. "Peruse the menu and make some choices. The server will be back any minute. Explanations can come later," she says, looking directly at James.

"Andy's agreed to drive us all back, haven't you, darling?"

"Yes, I'd be happy to."

The server appears with a tray on which are six complimentary hors d'oeuvres. "Have you had time to choose starters and mains yet, ladies, gentlemen?"

They all place their orders, which are carefully noted by the attentive server.

"Oh, these look good," says Louise.

"A little baked brie on a bed of grated beetroot and heritage carrot drizzled with the chef's secret balsamic chilli dressing. Enjoy."

"I mentioned you were veggie, Andy, as I knew there would be one or two extra dishes thrown in," says Mick.

"Very thoughtful, dear," says Louise.

"Thanks, Mick," adds Andy.

They tuck into the delightfully light brie.

James is wondering how soon he will make some excuse to join Lucy and Hilary and explain things. He knows Sally will be very reluctant to let him leave again, without an extremely convincing reason.

CHAPTER THIRTY

Lucy is fuming with James. Not only did he drag Andy off, almost as soon as she arrived, but he's now stolen Mick, too.

"I don't think this is what I was expecting when James asked me to come and present them with the bloody scrolls he made. Something's going on."

"Maybe it was my arrival that tipped him over the edge? Whilst it was… is… nice to see him, I always knew it might freak him out."

Andy's been AWOL for about ten minutes, and it must be five minutes since he dragged Mick away. I'm going to find them.

"Are you sure that's wise?"

"It beats sitting here like turkeys waiting for Christmas."

"We could just order for ourselves. I'm starving and reading the menu's got me salivating at the prospect. The server's just brought food to the couple at the next table. I'll grab his attention." She beckons and the server heads over. "Can the two of us order starters and mains please? I'm not sure where the chaps have got to, but the two of us are starving."

"I'll take your order with pleasure, ladies. I will also be back with an appetiser on the house."

"Sounds good," says Hilary.

"If they're not back here by the time we've finished the appetiser, I'm going looking for them."

"Okay. If they're not back by then, I'll come with you."

* * *

James decides he can't wait any longer. He can tell both Mick and Andy are getting increasingly anxious Lucy may appear at any moment. He determines he'll need to be honest with them about the unexpected arrival of their wives and clutches his stomach and makes to stand up.

"Dicky tummy," he says, "need to dash." He heads for the door to reception without looking back.

"I'm not buying this," says Sally, and before either Mick or Andy can think or act, she is on her feet and hurrying after him.

"James is acting rather strangely this evening, Mick. Is he alright?"

Mick decides the way the evening is going, there is no way Lucy's presence is going to remain a secret. "James had invited someone to join us this evening to present us with scrolls to commemorate the completion of our walk."

Andy immediately looks anxious. He hopes Lucy's play for him, and the provision of her address, will not form part of Mick's sudden conversion to truth telling.

"He invited someone else to dine with you? Who? Is that why he's like a cat on hot bricks?" asks Louise.

"He'd gone to meet them when he bumped into the three of you," says Andy.

"So, you're in on this, too?" says Melissa.

"Both Mick and I knew he had invited somebody,

but James wanted to keep it a secret from us until this evening."

"Whatever for?" says Louise.

"I expect he had his reasons," says Mick.

"Have you met this person?" says Melissa.

"It turns out to be someone we met whilst we were doing the walk. She showed a genuine interest in our journey," says Mick.

"She," says Louise. "You mean, you were all going to enjoy dining here with another woman?"

"Well, yes," says Andy.

"What's she called?" asks Melissa.

"What kind of woman would meet three men she's only met once, on her own, for a slap-up meal?" says Louise.

"She's not on her own," says Mick. "She's brought a friend with her."

"Has she?" says Andy, sounding confused.

"Her best friend's called Hilary, and she lives in Otley," says Mick.

"Otley," snaps Melissa. "Do you know this person?"

Andy shakes his head. "Of her, yes. Lucy told us about having a friend in Otley when we met her."

"It must have been a long and intimate conversation you had together if you were sharing details of friends," says Louise.

"Look, we've only met Lucy once, until tonight, and I don't even know what Hilary looks like," says Andy.

"So, if they're here, where the hell are they?" asks Melissa.

"I know where they are," says Louise. "I thought it was strange they ushered us into this dining room. Nice as it is, it doesn't quite match up to the grandeur of the main restaurant with the grand piano in the corner. Does it, Mick?"

"Er, no, dear."

"Right, come on, let's meet your two mystery dates."

Louise stands up and marches towards the door with Melissa in hot pursuit, whilst Mick and Andy exchange anxious looks.

"This evening's not exactly going as planned, is it, Mick? Melissa's about to explode, and Louise is a woman on a mission."

* * *

Sally catches sight of James disappearing into the restaurant, as she follows him into reception. Dicky tummy my foot, she thinks. There is an internal window to the right of the door, with voile curtains that don't completely obscure the restaurant from prying eyes. Sally peers through to locate James before charging into the room. It takes a little while to find him. He is still standing but is leaning over a large table at which two women are seated. They seem to argue. She tears herself away from the observed tableau and pushes open the door.

James has his back to her, so doesn't see her striding over to the table. He explains the unexpected arrival of the three wives, apologised profusely and suggested Lucy and Hilary stay and enjoy a meal together, on him, of course, before Sally gets to the table.

"I don't know who you two women are, nor do I care, but," turning to James she continues, "if you're not back in the other dining room in sixty seconds, you won't be going home with me tonight."

With that, Sally turns tail and heads back to reception.

"Sally, let me explain," says James. "That's Sally, my wife."

"So, I gathered," says Lucy.

"You'd better go," says Hilary.

"You've really ballsed this up, haven't you?" says Lucy.

"Perhaps we better go," says Hilary.

"No way. We'll enjoy our fine dining courtesy of your chump of a loverboy here."

"Steady on, Lucy, he wasn't to know, was he? After all, you thought it was okay to spring me on him."

"Yeh, you had to be dragged screaming and kicking."

Excuse me, I have to go," says James, turning and hurrying out of the room.

He doesn't see Hilary pick up a glass of water and throw it in Lucy's face. He hears a stifled scream.

* * *

Louise spots Sally leaving the restaurant and heading towards them.

"Sally, I know what's going on," Louise calls across the reception area.

"So do I," says Sally. "James is in there chatting to two women."

"Mick's just told us everything. It'll be Lucy and her friend Hilary."

"She's from Otley," says Melissa.

"Who the hell are Lucy and Hilary?" asks Sally.

"James invited Lucy to come and present them all with some commemorative scrolls he's had printed as mementos of the walk."

"What's so special about Lucy and why all the surrounding secretiveness?" says Sally. "Anyway, I've told James if he's not back with us all in sixty seconds, he won't be going home with me tonight."

The three women return to their table and re-join Mick and Andy.

"Everything all right?" asks Andy.

"Look, it's not what it looks like," says Mick, "James just wanted…"

"Shut up, Mick," says Sally. "I want the explanation from James. If he's not back in here in thirty seconds, I'm leaving."

"Yes," says Louise, "and you Mick are leaving with me, too."

"We'll come with you. Andy will need to drive us," adds Melissa.

The door opens and a somewhat flustered James heads towards them.

He sits down. "Explanations are called for and as it is definitely my fault Lucy is here and probably my fault Hilary's here, I should start talking."

"This better be good," says Sally.

"First, the idea to have scrolls printed to ratify the achievement of completing our somewhat alternative Coast to Coast was mine. Mick came up with the great idea of us dining here before setting off back home."

Louise smiles at hearing confirmation that eating at

the restaurant was Mick's idea.

"It was also my idea to invite someone to come and present the scrolls to us. I tried to think of someone who would be appropriate, and then I remembered Lucy and our conversation with her in Richmond. She was probably the one person who we met along the way..." Andy is looking worried.

Surely James will not detail the story of what actually happened in the cafe in Richmond?

However, James merely states, "We got into conversation with Lucy. She was interested in our journey, told us she had always meant to do it herself, but spent as much time living in France as in Richmond these days." He doesn't mention she gave them her address. "It seemed to me she was the ideal person to undertake the presentation."

Mick steps in. "It turns out she was a little wary of coming on her own and so invited her friend Hilary to come."

"She apparently lives near us in Otley," says Melissa, again looking questioningly at Andy.

* * *

Lucy recovers her composure after the shock of the cold water and is frantically mopping her face and neckline with her serviette. She looks at Hilary, smiles and then laughs.

"I suppose I asked for that," she says.

"We both thought it would be fun if I came along. You probably wouldn't have come on your own anyway," says Hilary.

"I wouldn't mind being a fly on the wall wherever the six of them are to hear James try to explain us," says Lucy.

"Poor lad."

"What if we just go through to them and help with the explanations?"

"Do you really think that's a good idea?" says Hilary.

"As long as we steer clear of your relationship with James, what harm can it do?"

"Well!"

"Go on, aren't you curious to see a bit more of the woman you're up against in soliciting James's attention?"

"Curious yes, but…"

"I'm certainly curious to find out more about Andy's wife."

"Okay, but if we are not welcome, let's just retreat quietly and enjoy the rest of the evening as two good friends having a fine dining experience together."

"At James's expense."

"I feel guilty about that. Perhaps we should just…"

"He offered, I've accepted. End of."

The two women explain to the server they are hoping to join friends in the other dining room and their orders should be brought through to them there, but not to clear their table, as accommodating them in the other dining room may not be possible.

CHAPTER THIRTY-ONE

The server comes to take their starter plates away, including James's untouched ham hock tureen.

"James kept the identity of the scroll presenter quiet from me and Andy," says Mick, "although we almost got it out of him last night, when he let slip it was a woman we all knew. I can understand why he chose Lucy. She expressed an interest in our walk and a desire to do something similar."

Andy is relieved Lucy making eyes at him in Richmond has not come out.

Sally looks up at the two women she now knows to be Lucy and Hilary approaching.

"Excuse us, I hope you don't mind us coming through to speak with you," says Lucy. "I can understand how us being here to dine with your husbands may look, particularly to you, Sally.

Sally still smells a rat, but isn't sure why. She asks, "How did you", addressing James, "know how to contact Lucy, if you don't mind me asking?"

Mick steps in to support his friend. "Lucy gave us her address when we met her in Richmond. As she is often in France, the cottage she has there is often empty and available."

"I told them, if they were ever planning to be walking via Richmond again to check out with me beforehand," says Lucy.

Andy confirms Mick and Lucy's story.

"Do you often chat up strange men in cafes in Richmond?" asks Sally.

"And write your address and give it to them?" adds Melissa.

"It's actually the only time I've ever done it," says Lucy, feeling uncomfortable.

"Maybe you and I better just leave," says Hilary.

The server and the Duty Manager present themselves. "I understand these two ladies are to join you and we may need to add an extra table to facilitate this," says the Duty Manager.

"I don't think that would be a good idea," says Louise.

Sally is sensing James's discomfiture. "Why not join us? We can play at being one big happy family, can't we?"

"Is that wise?" asks James.

"Was it wise to invite two virtual strangers to dine with you at a celebratory meal?" says Sally.

"Inviting Hilary was my idea," says Lucy. "It was also a means of being able to drive them all back home afterwards, to maximise their time here."

"So, let me be clear, a woman who was a virtual stranger was joining you for dinner and another woman who was a complete stranger was driving you all back home?" says Melissa.

"Girls, this was supposed to be…" says James.

"Don't patronise, James," interjects Sally.

"…a bit of a celebration for us finishing our challenge walk."

"Look," says Mick. "Nobody had any bad intentions.

We are all here. Perhaps we can just try to make the mo..."

"Mick, you've said too much already," says Louise. "Having a meal to celebrate is one thing, but inviting two women you hardly know to join you is quite another."

"Are we sure they hardly know them?" says Sally.

"What are you insinuating?" responds Lucy.

"Well, it just doesn't cut with me," says Sally.

"It's just as James and Lucy explained," says Andy.

"James and... Lucy, is it?" says Melissa, picking up from Sally.

"Don't be silly, you'll be putting two and two together and suggesting Hilary and I in a minute, just because she lives in Otley."

"Well, is it?"

"Is it what?"

"You and Hilary?"

"Absolutely not," says Andy. "I've only just met her."

James can see the evening disintegrating before his eyes. What's more, there's another four courses still to go.

"I take full responsibility. Maybe it was a silly idea to invite Lucy to come and present the scrolls to the three of us. Clearly with the three of you here, too, it's become an even sillier idea. I'm sure Lucy and Hilary feel incredibly uncomfortable. I know I do."

"And so you should," says Sally.

"Excuse me. Are we converting you into an eight-table setting or not?" asks the Duty Manager, who has been standing patiently by whilst conversation has continued.

"Yes," says Sally emphatically.

Lucy picks up her story. "It is as James says. I met the guys in a cafe in Richmond. They had about half an hour to kill before the bus to Darlington. I overheard them talking about walking the Coast to Coast and got into conversation with them. When James contacted me with his proposal about this evening, I was a little reluctant at first to meet three chaps I'd only met once before, but then I thought if I have a friend with me it will be another opportunity to discuss the details of their walk and kind of be part of their success in completing it, so I agreed."

"How come you three came up to Saltburn?" says James, trying now to steer the conversation away from Lucy.

"Well," says Sally, "Louise knew the restaurant you were all coming to, said it was excellent and wouldn't it be fun if we all came up to surprise you, celebrate you finishing the challenge and then give you all a lift back home."

Sally is still taking in James and Lucy's comments. Their main courses arrive at this point and are placed in front of each of them.

Louise reminds Mick of when they had dined at the restaurant before.

"Very romantic," says Lucy.

"Mick has his moments, don't you, love?" says Louise.

Mick smiles sheepishly.

"When was the last time you took me out for a five-star meal, James?" asks Sally.

"Yes, Andy, it's a while since we shared such an experience," says Melissa.

James says, "I've said this is all my fault. But, between the eight of us, we have a table at this fine restaurant and we're all here to enjoy a five-course meal. The one course we've had so far has been peppered with interruptions, barbed comments and false accusations…"

Sally seeks to interject again, but James stands up, raises his voice, and carries on. "I totally accept responsibility for the situation we are in, and apologise unreservedly for my actions, however well intentioned. So, have a go at me, but please no-one else."

He sits down. Hillary feels like applauding, but decides that would be inappropriate.

Lucy addresses Sally, Louise and Melissa. "I totally understand you being uncomfortable with us being here as part of the celebrations for your three husbands having completed such a splendid walk. Hilary and I are perfectly happy to leave before the next course. The six of you can enjoy the rest of your evening together."

"I appreciate your gesture," says Mick, adding, "but that said, I would like you both to stay.

"Shall we just enjoy the food in front of us and review the situation after our mains? I'm salivating at the prospect of tucking into this roasted vegetable wellington," says Andy.

An uneasy and wary silence descends over the table as all focus on eating.

"How did you discover this place, Mick?" asks Lucy.

"He didn't. Some friends of ours did," says Louise, "and we dined here first with them."

"What made you think Mick discovered it?" asks Sally.

"James told me Mick recommended it to Andy and him."

Sally is becoming increasingly convinced James and Lucy have much more in common than one casual meeting in a cafe.

"What else has James shared with you?"

"Sally, I thought we'd agreed to just focus on enjoying the wonderful food," says James.

"Maybe," says Sally, "but I still want an answer to my question."

"The one meeting you all know about and maybe two or three phone calls to discuss tonight's gathering," says Lucy.

"No secret meetings in Otley, whilst visiting your friend?"

"Absolutely not."

"Only, James has previous for unexplained chunks of time in Otley. Haven't you, darling?" She directs the last remark at James.

Louise is immediately interested. "You left Melissa and Andy's Tour de France party very early. Didn't he, Melissa?"

"I seem to recall you did."

"I've already told you I went into Otley to savour the atmosphere in the town on what was a very special day."

James is feeling increasingly uncomfortable and wishes Lucy and Hilary had stayed put in the other dining room.

"Hilary and I will just finish this course and then leave. It's clear you are extremely uncomfortable with our presence and are determined to make two and two add up to five and provoke a reaction."

"That may be best," says Mick. "I know I encouraged you to stay earlier, but I regret that."

"What do you do, Hilary?" asks Melissa.

"I'm a yoga teacher, actually."

"Really? Andy has the ambition to turn to teaching yoga when he's pensioned off from his current job."

"Small world, isn't it?" says Sally.

"He's done a lot of online training," says Melissa.

"He just needs to find an experienced teacher to provide some peer reviewing of his practice then," says Hilary.

"Oh, he tells me he's been seeing someone in that capacity over the past few months, haven't you, Andy?"

"I have, a bloke based in Ilkley," says Andy.

Melissa is absolutely convinced it is a woman in Otley who is providing such peer support. *And what else?* she wonders.

"It's you, isn't it?" she shrieks.

She flings the remaining contents of her glass at Hilary.

"You're absolutely deranged and completely wrong," says Hilary, mopping herself with a napkin. "Come on, Lucy."

Lucy makes to stand up and James stands up, too.

"I'll see them to their car. I feel responsible for this. You are wrong though, Melissa."

"Sit down," says Sally, "or you won't be travelling home with us tonight."

"It's alright James, we're big girls, we can find our way to the car, thank you," says Lucy. Turning, as she heads for the door, she points at Melissa, "Unlike you."

Hilary makes to follow Lucy, hesitates, picks up the water jug and pours the contents over Melissa's head. Melissa shrieks and Andy rises to wrestle the jug away before it is completely empty.

"Come on, Mick, we're going," says Louise.

Melissa, having regained her composure, is making to run after Hilary and Andy has to cling on to her and gets a cuff round the head for his troubles. James dashes off to ensure Lucy and Hilary get safely off the premises, before he returns to help Andy in keeping Melissa from going after them.

"Let's just all go back and try to finish our meal in peace," says a red-faced and somewhat breathless James.

"You can do what you want," says Sally, "but we are all going home, and you can go to hell."

They all head out of the restaurant. James is still trying to get them to see sense. He is about to follow them into the car park when the Duty Manager grabs his arm.

"Excuse me sir, there is the bill to pay. After paying the £301.89 bill, he goes outside again, but there is no sign of either his two walking buddies, the three wives, or Lucy and Hilary.

He returns to reception and over to the bar, where the friendly barman is still in attendance.

He smiles wistfully and says, "Talisker please."

"I'm sorry sir, the Duty Manager has clarified neither you nor any of your party are to be served or are welcome here. If I were you, I would go, sir. If he sees you in here, he's going to be annoyed."

"I'll just collect my stuff from the cloakroom."

"Everything was packed into the back of the Touran, sir."

James heads back out into the car park just as the rain falls. Turning up the collar on his shirt, he leaves the grounds of the Brockley Hall, turns left onto Glenside, and starts walking.

Peter Kay

FIRST MAYOR OF RICHMOND

T'was sixteen hundred and six,
for legend has it so,
when, whilst out hunting all alone,
Robert Willance, future mayor
of Richmond, shattered his femur bone.

His horse, a noble steed of some renown
had always borne him well,
but as November's dense mists thronged,
the bewildered beast bolted,
racing headlong into nothingness.

With Willance clinging on for life,
his horse plunged to its death,
two hundred feet o'er Whitcliffe Scar.
Robert lay prostrate, right leg broken,
twisted, breached, death's door ajar.

With no prospect of immediate respite,
he slit soft belly of his beloved horse,
using a trusted hunting knife. No malice.
Plunged his leg in up to groin and hilt,
to try and keep it for his balance.

For two days he held on to life and limb,
before rescue came at last.

A Very Alternative Coast to Coast

Alas whilst Robert survived, his poor leg
could not be saved, t'was buried
with due ceremony, in his chosen grave.

T'was sixteen hundred and eight
when brave Willance and his stump,
became first mayor of Richmond.
Eight long years, without a single blunder,
Before dying, reight well, in his slumber.

And so it came to pass that in his death requited,
Robert Willance and his leg were gladly reunited.

This Poem was written by the author, based on a story, researched by him and contained within A Very Alternative Coast to Coast. It was first published in April 2021 on the website – 'Spilling Cocoa Over Martin Amis.'

Peter Kay

ABOUT THE AUTHOR

Peter has been writing for the past twelve years, following retirement from full time employment. His first book, *A Pennine Way Odyssey*, was published in 2012. His second, *Show Me The Way To Santiago*, was published in 2020. Both those books were written as Travel memoirs.

He also writes, flash fiction, short stories, monologues, children's books and poetry. He has had a monologue performed at A Leeds LitFest, a short story read on BBC Radio Leeds. A piece of his flash fiction and several of his poems, including the one in the book, have also been published.

A Very Alternative Coast To Coast is his first venture into writing a fictional novel.

A Children's book, illustrated by his eldest daughter, Rebecca, is set to be published in the near future.

He is currently working on a murder mystery story set in Yorkshire in the 1930s.

Lightning Source UK Ltd.
Milton Keynes UK
UKHW011154130622
404347UK00002B/129